MW01595005

Christian Perspectives on the Modern World

Where Does the Church Go from Here?

Charles E. Cravey

In His Steps Publishing

ISBN: 978-1-58535-065-0 (PRINT)

ISBN: 978-1-58535-066-7 (EPUB)

Library of Congress Catalog Control Number: 2025902502

All scriptures are from the King James Version of the Holy Bible

Printed in the United States and published by:

IN HIS STEPS PUBLISHING, Statesboro, Georgia

Contents

Dedication:

To my dear friend and colleague,

The Rev. Dr. Marvin Terry Deloach.

You've been a dear and loyal friend for so many years.

Foreword

This book has been fifty-two years in the making! It has taken that long for me to gather the experience, the knowledge, and the fortitude to write on this precious issue in our lives today: THE CHURCH!

The church has been my first love since I accepted Christ as my Lord and Savior at eighteen. Before that, I always thought that I believed in God as a child and believed in Santa Claus.

Right after graduating high school, I attended a medical laboratory technician school in Atlanta, Georgia. Following that training, I returned home to find a job waiting for me with Juvenile Court Services as a community worker, the first such in the state of Georgia. Knowing that I was going into full-time ministry, I served in the capacity of community worker until I completed my license to preach studies. I eventually received my first church and began college training. I made my way from ABAC (Abraham Baldwin Agricultural College) in Tifton, Georgia, to Georgia Southern College in Statesboro, Georgia. After receiving my B.S. in Sociology from Southern, I began studies at the Candler School of Theology at Emory University in Atlanta. Following a transfer to Trinity Theological Seminary, I received an M.S.L. and a Ph.D. in theology. During that time, I also completed eight summer semesters at Emory, satisfying the Board of Ordained Ministry.

I have always been a writer since an early age. My poetry began at five, and journaling began shortly thereafter. I love to write and have dedicated my life to writing music, composing church anthems, and writing newspaper and magazine columns. The book you now hold is #30 in an extensive line of published books, which God gave me the ability to compile. I hope you find something within these pages that will better your life. If so, then my work will be done.

God bless you on your journey today.

The Rev. Dr. Charles E. Cravey, 2025

Introduction

It is crucial to examine faith in the modern world. In the modern world, where people are increasingly more secular and the world is becoming more technological, the search for meaning and purpose has become an essential task. Many people are struggling with questions of existence and finding comfort and guidance in the uncertain world. Exploring faith offers a chance to examine some of the most fundamental philosophical and spiritual issues and to find responses, to find comfort in belonging, and to develop a better understanding of themselves and their place in the world.

Faith acts as a moral compass to help navigate the complexities of a society in the modern world. Many such communities are also sources of support and solidarity; they provide a sense of belonging in an individualistic world. Therefore, the current trends in the world make it essential to explore faith because such an exploration is necessary for the satisfaction of human needs and the creation of a framework for personal growth and society's harmony.

I will explore in Chapter One the role of faith in crisis. Faith, which is often private and sometimes spiritual, can be a crucial element in coping with and overcoming challenging times. Throughout this chapter, I will examine how faith can serve as a source of comfort, guidance, and hope during times of crisis. Through personal stories and scholarly research, I will explore the impact of faith on individuals and groups, including how different religious and philosophical traditions shape one's understanding of faith in the face of adversity.

I will also examine potential challenges and doubts arising from tests of faith and how individuals find strength and resilience in their beliefs. In examining the complex interactions between faith and the human experience, this chapter aims to contribute to the understanding of the multifaceted nature of faith in crisis.

In Chapter Two, we will delve into the topic of persecution and its impact on modern society. We will examine the experiences of those persecuted for their religious, political, or social beliefs. We will examine various forms of persecution, including religious, political, and social persecution, and look at the causes of such persecution. Modern-day martyrs, those who died for their principles and ideas, will be the focus of our exploration. Through case studies and personal accounts, we will look at the courage and resilience of these modern-day martyrs and the effect of their actions on the understanding of justice and human rights. By relating these powerful stories, we hope to increase people's understanding of the importance of religious freedom and the ongoing fight against today's persecution.

In Chapter Three of this study, we will look at environmental stewardship. Responsible and sustainable management of natural resources and ecosystems ensures their long-term sustainability. This chapter will examine why environmental stewardship is important in fixing the problems caused by humans in the environment and in promoting conservation efforts. It will discuss how individuals, organizations, and governments can become better environmental stewards. The chapter will also look at case studies and success stories of environmental stewardship initiatives around the world and how these might serve as models for implementation in other regions. This comprehensive exploration of the subject will leave the reader with a better understanding of the importance of environmental stewardship and the knowledge and tools needed to help preserve and protect our planet.

In Chapter Four, we will explore social justice and human rights from a complex and interconnected perspective. These issues are truly relevant in the contemporary world because they relate to the basic concepts of equality, fairness, and human dignity. We will discuss various dimensions of social justice, including economic, political, and cultural aspects, and how they relate to human rights. Through a critical analysis of case studies, we will examine the challenges, and the progress made towards achieving social justice and upholding human rights, both globally and at specific locations. By doing this, we aim to increase people's understanding of the principles and the laws that govern social justice and human rights and the importance of these for creating a just society.

Chapter Five is about technology, ethics, and digital evangelism. This chapter will examine the ethical issues that arise from technology and its use in everyday life. It will explore how technology can support or challenge moral principles and how to think about the ethical questions of digital evangelism. The chapter will also look at the role of technology in the dissemination of religious ideas and possible ethical dilemmas. This comprehensive analysis of these topics offers the document an in-depth understanding of the role technology, ethics, and digital evangelism play in our modern world.

Chapter Six of our study is on cultural connections and their impact on pop culture. In this chapter, we will analyze how diverse cultures influence and shape popular culture. We will examine how the interaction and exchange of cultural ideas, customs, and traditions shape aspects of modern pop culture. From music and fashion and from cultural icons and symbols, this chapter will examine the dynamics of cultural flows. Through case studies, interviews, and extensive research, we will try to understand the nature of cultural borrowing and appropriation, including cross-pollination, and the effects of cultural connections.

In Chapter Seven, which is entitled "Global Missions and Healthcare," we will embark on a fascinating journey of international missions in healthcare. This chapter aims to make the reader understand the various aspects of global healthcare missions, the challenges that come with them, the impact of such missions, and how they can be effective. We will also look at the role of healthcare professionals such as doctors, nurses, and other medical volunteers in helping to meet the healthcare needs of target communities. In addition, we will examine the importance of cultural sensitivity, communication, and other ethical considerations that are involved in global healthcare missions. By the end of the chapter, the reader should be able to understand the steps to take to participate in this mission efficiently.

Chapter Eight is a collection of personal stories and testimonies that describe noteworthy events or transitional processes. These narratives contain topics such as overcoming adversity, personal growth and self-discovery, triumphs and challenges, and moments of inspiration. We will present these personal stories to help readers relate to them and understand the themes and concepts of this study.

Chapter Nine is about the future of the church. In this chapter, we will look at the challenges and opportunities that the church will face in the coming years. We shall examine the changes in the religious and spiritual landscape of the world and how these are likely to affect the role of the Church in society. We shall also examine the developing needs and desires of the faithful and how they relate to issues of inclusivity and social justice in the modern world.

As we walk the faith journey together, every Christian has the responsibility to promote restorative justice, foster reconciliation, and hold on to hope for the future. It is not just a suggestion; it is a divine duty to which God has called us to respond to the world He has created and put into our care. Our responsibility goes beyond our personal spiritual growth; it extends to the well-being of our communities, the mending of broken relationships, and the improvement of the world for all. In answering this call, we are called to be agents of change, striving for justice for the oppressed, extending forgiveness to the hurtful, and spreading hope in the dark. By actively engaging in restorative justice, we effect change on individuals, communities, and societies. Our faith compels us to work towards a world where love, compassion, and understanding reign, where justice is served, and where hope shines in the darkest of times. Therefore, we should embrace our role in this ongoing journey towards a more just, reconciled, and hopeful future.

While I was in my early twenties, I spent almost three years as a community worker (my official title) with the State Department of Juvenile Court Services. This position required me to work with juvenile delinquents who had broken the law and were standing on the wrong side of justice. Some of my responsibilities included collecting data from them, making home assessments, working with their local schools, and transporting them to court, to a mental health clinic, or to local detention centers.

I could just as easily spend time with these young individuals and take them to Atlanta Braves' games in Atlanta, to theme parks in the area, and to other recreational activities to develop camaraderie with them. These outings helped break down the 'legal' facade and establish a connection because I had previously broken the law and paid my own dues in years past. I had been a direct beneficiary of the system.

What I have seen while working with children in poor environments is the powerful effect of providing them with opportunities to enlarge their horizons. I have been in their shoes; I have understood their plight, and I have developed a strong bond with them. The arduous work that goes into shaping these children, many from broken homes, is a rewarding and fulfilling process because I have seen positive changes in their everyday lives. They have gained a new sense of hope and a way to overcome their unique challenges.

Most of the children that I had the privilege of working with were from poor families, living in poverty, and lacking resources. Their limited environment restricts their opportunities, dreams, and aspirations. I have experienced similar circumstances, and I feel for them and want to help change their lives.

As a former beneficiary of programs aimed at supporting underprivileged youth, I felt an intense sense of duty to give back and help break the cycle of poverty. By sharing my story of overcoming adversity, I aimed to inspire and empower these children, showing them, they too could overcome their challenges and achieve their dreams. This personal connection fueled my passion for the work and provided a powerful motivation to make a lasting impact on their lives. Since these children have multiple and complex problems, I dedicated my time to engaging with them in every way I could. The joy that comes with seeing them steadily improve is worth the demanding work that goes into it. Each day brings with it the possibility of a change in their attitudes, outlooks, and abilities. Through various educational and mentoring initiatives, we have provided them with the support to enable them to manage their circumstances and strive for a better future.

The most significant impact of our work has been the generation of hope among these children. Many of them believe that there is no way out of their current situation and that they can never improve their lives. But through exposure to new experiences, educational opportunities, and positive role models, they see a way out of their dilemmas. This newly found hope serves as a catalyst for change, making them more determined to overcome obstacles and pursue their dreams.

Working with underprivileged children and seeing them grow and change has been a blessed honor. We have been able to provide them with the opportunity to see the world in a different light and to believe in themselves and their capacity to overcome adversity. Our tireless efforts have made these children believe that they have a future and that they have a say in helping to change the world. This work gave me excellent job satisfaction, and I remain committed to continuing this process not just for these children but for all underprivileged children across the globe.

From that transformation, I realized God called me to a lifelong ministry of service to all people. I have spent the past 52 years of my life as a pastor, serving churches eagerly. These last 52 years I have devoted myself entirely to this office, spending my time, energy, and passion in guiding and supporting congregations. It is a vocation which has become inseparable from my very being, defining my identity and purpose in life. Retrospectively, I am not retired; I have always had a desire to serve others and help humankind. Retirement is a term that implies stepping back and staying out of the action, but my passion to make a positive difference in the world has only grown stronger.

Every day offers new opportunities to comfort, inspire, and uplift those in need, and I am grateful to continue this sacred work until the end of my days.

Are you ready to discover ways to serve? Then this book is for you.

The Rev. Dr. Charles E. Cravey, 2025

1

The Role of Faith in Crisis

A T THE TIME OF this writing, former President Jimmy Carter, age 100, has passed away. It was a major milestone because few people live that long. A peanut farmer from Plains, Georgia, he rose to become the 39th U.S. President (1977-1981). Plains, a small southwestern Georgian town, was Carter's birthplace on October 1, 1924. From a humble farming family background, he later served in the U.S. Navy during World War II.

After his military service, Carter returned to Plains and took over the family peanut business. His involvement in community affairs led him to politics, and he eventually became the Governor of Georgia in 1971. Significant domestic and international challenges marked Carter's presidency, including the energy crisis, the Iran hostage crisis, and the Soviet invasion of Afghanistan. Despite many obstacles, he committed himself to human rights, environmental conservation, and promoting world peace. After leaving the office, Carter dedicated himself to various philanthropic endeavors, including his work with Habitat for Humanity. His passing marks the end of an era, but his legacy as a compassionate leader and advocate for social justice will continue to inspire generations to come. The world, not just the United States, has lost perhaps the best representative we have for world peace, feeding the needy, and reaching out to everyone.

We have just had elections, and Donald Trump defeated Kamala Harris to serve as our next president. He is the exact polar opposite of Jimmy Carter in terms of political ideology, leadership style, and policy priorities. Unlike Jimmy Carter, who emphasized human rights, diplomacy, and environmental conservation, Donald Trump built his political career on economic growth, national security, and immigration reform. Their personal backgrounds and experiences also differ. The presidency saw Jimmy Carter, a former peanut farmer from Georgia, display a humble and down-to-earth demeanor, in contrast to Donald Trump, a wealthy entrepreneur and reality TV star, known for his flamboyant personality and opulent lifestyle. With these contrasting characteristics, the election of Donald Trump marks a significant shift in the direction and tone of the country's leadership, not to mention the fact that he is now a convicted felon who will not serve any time!

There is also a war being raged by Russia against Ukraine:

The ongoing conflict has become a major global concern, as it continues to claim the lives of innocent civilians and soldiers on both sides. This conflict, which was instigated by Russia, has escalated into a full-fledged war, causing immense suffering and devastation. In this chapter, we will delve into the background of the conflict, the causes behind it, and the dire consequences it has had on the people living in these regions.

Background:

The political unrest in Ukraine during 2014 caused the conflict between Russia and Ukraine. The Ukrainian government's decision to pursue closer ties with the European Union sparked widespread protests, leading to the eventual ousting of the pro-Russian President Viktor Yanukovych. Russia, viewing this as a threat to its influence in the region, swiftly annexed Crimea, a strategically important peninsula in Ukraine. The international community condemned this move, leading to a series of economic sanctions against Russia.

Causes and Escalation:

The annexation of Crimea by Russia marked the beginning of a broader conflict, with pro-Russian separatists rising in eastern Ukraine. These separatists, backed by Russia, seized control of key cities and territories, which the Ukrainian government vehemently opposed. Fierce separatist resistance met the Ukrainian government's attempts to regain control of these regions, escalating the conflict into a full-blown war.

Intense fighting, artillery shelling, and aerial bombardment has characterized the war, resulting in significant loss of life and destruction of infrastructure. Both sides have accused each other of various human rights violations and war crimes, including the targeting of civilians and the use of banned weapons. The conflict has created a humanitarian crisis, with thousands of people displaced from their homes and in desperate need of help. Trump proposes a peace deal where Ukraine gives up land seized by Russia, effectively condoning Russia's violent territorial gains. Would that be justice? Where is the love of God in all of this?

The consequences of this conflict have been devastating. This conflict has claimed thousands of innocent lives, injuring and traumatizing countless others. The war has also resulted in a severe economic downturn for both countries, with infrastructure, industries, and agricultural sectors suffering significant damage. The conflict has strained diplomatic relations between Russia and the international community, leading to political tensions and sanctions.

With no immediate resolution, the escalating war between Russia and Ukraine rages on. The toll it has taken on the people and the region is immeasurable. The international community's efforts to broker a peaceful resolution have achieved limited success so far. As the conflict persists, it is crucial to raise awareness and support initiatives that aim to alleviate the suffering and bring about a sustainable solution to this humanitarian crisis.

Today, a shocking news flash has brought to light a horrifying incident that unfolded on Bourbon Street in New Orleans. Reports state that a radicalized U.S. veteran intentionally drove his pickup truck into crowds on Bourbon Street, killing fourteen and injuring dozens.

As the details of this tragic event continue to emerge, some news stations have suggested a connection between the perpetrator and radical Islamist ideologies. Adding to the gravity of the situation, witnesses saw an ISIS flag prominently displayed on the back of his truck, raising concerns about potential extremist involvement. The motive behind this appalling act remains unclear, and authorities are currently investigating to understand the full extent of the circumstances of this devastating incident. Pure evil has been unleashed upon the world!

The Middle East region is currently witnessing a dire and intensifying conflict between Israelis and Palestinians. The longstanding disputes and grievances between these two sides have erupted into a full-scale war, resulting in widespread devastation and loss of innocent lives. This article aims to summarize the recent developments in this conflict, shedding light on the escalating violence and the involvement of various regional actors.

In response to the killing of innocent Jews at a concert and the seizing of hostages by Palestine, Israel has launched a series of retaliatory attacks on Gaza. These strikes, aimed at Hamas targets, have caused significant damage to infrastructure and resulted in a considerable number of casualties. Israel justifies these actions as necessary measures to protect its citizens and deter further acts of violence.

Adding another layer of complexity to the conflict, Iran has become increasingly involved in supporting the Palestinian cause. This has prompted Israel to expand its military operations beyond Gaza, targeting sections of Lebanon, Syria, and Iran itself. These actions further exacerbate tensions in the region and increase the risk of wider regional entanglement.

As the situation continues to deteriorate, the United States finds itself increasingly drawn into the conflict. Historically, a staunch ally of Israel, the U.S., now faces the challenging task of balancing its support for its longstanding partner while also attempting to de-escalate the situation and promote peace in the region. Resolving the Israeli-Palestinian conflict peacefully will depend heavily on the United States' mediating role.

With retaliatory attacks and regional actors involved, the Israeli-Palestinian conflict has entered a perilous and critical stage, potentially escalating into a wider regional conflict. The escalating violence and increasing involvement of various parties demand urgent attention and diplomatic efforts to halt the bloodshed and find a lasting solution. As the world watches this devastating conflict unfold, the hope for a peaceful resolution and the restoration of stability in the region remains paramount. Will there be peace? Will there ever be peace in that region of the world?

Years ago, I walked the streets of Jerusalem, down the Via Dolorosa, and witnessed children at a street crossing actively tossing rocks at each other. Our tour guide told us it was Palestinian and Jewish children, and they were a daily nuisance. Their rocks will become bombs and gunfire one day unless we can help bring about a lasting peace for both. Can't we all just get along?

Where is the Church?

When I ask this question, it is with bated breath that I tell you it is absent. There is a war going on in today's church as well, a clash of ideologies and beliefs. On one side, we have evangelical Christians who appear to be "holier than Thou", passionately advocating for a return to an earlier period in America. They long for a time when traditional values held sway and Christianity played a central role in society. On the other side, we find fundamentalist liberals who are equally fervent in their pursuit of progress and inclusivity. They strive to break free from the constraints of traditionalism, supporting the rights and freedoms of "everyone". These two factions stand in stark opposition, their differences fueling a heated debate within the church.

Where is the love of Christ expressed in John 3:16? In this famous verse, it states, "For God so loved the world that he gave his one and only Son, that whoever believes in him shall not perish but have eternal life." This verse reveals the depth of God's love for humanity. It showcases the sacrificial nature of love, as God willingly gave up his Son for the salvation of humankind. This act of love shows God's desire for a restored relationship with humanity and the offer of eternal life through faith in Jesus Christ.

John 3:16 remains relevant today, reminding us of God's immeasurable love, the hope, and eternal life found in Christ. It serves as a powerful reminder of the love that Christians are called to embody and share with others.

That love is not as clear in today's church as it should be. We are at war internally and externally, ignoring the commands of the Savior of the world. This lack of love and unity has given rise to various splinter groups within the church, each with its own interpretations and priorities. One such group is the Church of Nones, which comprises individuals who identify as religiously unaffiliated or having no specific religious affiliation. This group often emerged as a response to the perceived hypocrisy and lack of genuine love within traditional religious institutions. The Church of Nones seeks to create a community that embraces spirituality without the constraints or dogmas of organized religion. With a focus on individualism and personal beliefs, this group challenges the conventional notions of what it means to be part of a religious community. However, it is important to recognize that the rise of such splinter groups reflects the growing dissatisfaction with the lack of love, acceptance, and inclusivity within the broader church.

What does all of this tell us about our churches today? We are in real trouble with no clear-cut way out unless we stop our radicalized tom-foolery and return to the REAL CHURCH! The current state of our churches reflects a concerning trend towards radicalization and deviance from the true principles and values of the faith. This deviation from the core teachings has led to a multitude of issues plaguing our communities. From the erosion of moral values to the exploitation of vulnerable individuals, these problems are symptomatic of a departure from the authentic purpose and mission of the church. It is imperative that we acknowledge the gravity of the situation and take immediate action to rectify the course.

This entails a collective effort to refocus on the fundamental principles of love, compassion, and spiritual growth, which should be at the heart of any genuine church. By returning to these core values and discarding the radicalized ideologies that have infiltrated our congregations, we can rebuild a stronger, more inclusive, and morally upright church community. It is crucial that we engage in critical self-reflection, reevaluate our practices, and foster an environment that encourages open dialogue, respect, and understanding. Only through this concerted effort can we hope to reclaim the essence of the REAL CHURCH and restore faith in our religious institutions.

I attend a traditional protestant church called First United Methodist, in the heart of our small town. The church has been a pillar of our community for decades, providing spiritual guidance and a sense of belonging to its members. I have been a part of this congregation for a year now and have truly grown to love it. The warm and welcoming atmosphere, the beautiful hymns and music that resonate through the sanctuary, and the insightful sermons have all played a significant role in deepening my faith. I am a retired minister and have witnessed all of this in my 52 years of ministry.

In recent years, I have witnessed a significant shift within our church community. A more conservative faction has emerged, prompting sufficient members to leave and join this new group. The catalyst for this division was a long-standing debate that had been raging within our church for over fifty years - whether to ordain homosexuals as ministers, elders, and deacons.

This issue struck at the very core of our church's identity and teachings. It became a topic of heated discussions, passionate arguments, and fervent prayers. As someone who believes in the inclusive and accepting nature of Christianity, it broke my heart to witness the division that ensued. I could not help but question where the love of God was in all of this.

The split within our church was not just a matter of differing opinions; it felt like a fracture in the very foundation of our faith community. The sense of unity and togetherness that once bound us seemed to dissipate, replaced by a palpable tension and a growing sense of division.

It is disheartening to see a church that had always preached love, compassion, and acceptance become a battleground for such a divisive issue. The very essence of

Christianity - the teachings of Jesus Christ to love one another unconditionally seemed to be overshadowed by the focus on sexual orientation.

In times like these, it is important to remember that the love of God transcends human disagreements and divisions. It is a love that embraces all, regardless of sexual orientation or any other characteristic that may set us apart. As I continue to navigate this challenging period in my beloved church, I believe God's love will ultimately bring about unity and understanding.

Historical Examples:

In times of historical crisis, faith communities have often been the primary providers of relief, support, and hope for those affected. The following are some key examples:

1. **Plagues**: During pandemics like the Black Death in the 14th century or the more recent Spanish Flu in 1918-1919, faith communities have played a crucial role in providing spiritual support, healthcare, and aid to the affected individuals. Churches, mosques, temples, and other places of worship have transformed into makeshift hospitals and shelters, offering a haven for the ill and dying. These religious institutions have not only

served as physical spaces to treat the ill but also as sources of solace and comfort during times of immense suffering. Religious leaders and members of their communities have helped people affected by the plagues by offering comfort, prayers, and advice. In addition, religious organizations have organized relief efforts, distributing food, medicine, and other essential supplies to the affected communities. Their compassionate response during times of crisis has shown the power of faith in fostering resilience and unity in the face of adversity.

2. **Wars**: In times of conflict, such as World Wars I and II, faith groups have played pivotal roles in various aspects of war efforts. These religious organizations have acted as mediators, providing a platform for dialogue and negotiations between warring factions, often working tirelessly to bring about peaceful resolutions. They have been crucial in providing much-needed humanitarian aid, helping both soldiers and civilians affected by the devastation of war. Religious groups have also

played significant roles in offering spiritual solace to those affected by the horrors of war, providing a source of comfort and solace during such trying times. These organizations have conducted rescue missions, bravely venturing into war zones to save lives and help those in need. They have also been instrumental in helping refugees and displaced persons, offering them shelter, food, and support to help rebuild their lives in the aftermath of war. Throughout history, faith groups have showed their unwavering commitment to peace, compassion, and service to humanity during times of war.

3. **Natural Disasters**: In the aftermath of hurricanes, earthquakes, and other natural disasters, faith communities are among the first responders. For instance, churches played a crucial role in providing aid and shelter during Hurricane Katrina in 2005. In New Orleans, where the hurricane caused widespread devastation and displacement, churches opened their doors to provide temporary housing for those who had lost their homes.

They also organized volunteer efforts to distribute food, water, and other essential supplies to affected individuals. Faith-based organizations collaborated with local authorities and relief agencies to coordinate rescue operations and provide emotional support to traumatized survivors. These faith communities showed their commitment to serving others during times of crisis, exemplifying the values of compassion and solidarity that are central to many religious traditions. The efforts of these organizations and individuals highlight the important role that faith communities can play in disaster response and recovery.

4. **Civil Unrest:** During periods of social turmoil, such as the civil rights movements in the 1960s, faith leaders from various religious organizations played a crucial role in advocating for justice, peace, and reconciliation. They actively participated in the fight against racial discrimination and organized peaceful protests to raise awareness of systemic inequality and injustice. Faith leaders provided sanctuary for those seeking refuge

from violence and supported communities that were torn apart by acts of brutality. Through their efforts, they helped rebuild trust and fostered a sense of unity among diverse groups of people.

5. **Public Health Emergencies:** Faith communities have consistently shown their willingness to collaborate with government agencies and non-profit organizations in times of public health emergencies. These collaborations aim to provide a coordinated and effective response to crises such as disease outbreaks, natural disasters, and other emergencies that affect public health. Faith leaders often leverage their influence and resources to raise awareness about preventative measures, promote vaccination campaigns, and offer support to affected individuals and communities. By working together, faith communities and other stakeholders can address public health challenges more comprehensively and ensure the well-being of their congregants and the wider society. Guides and resources specifically designed to engage with faith-based responders, such as the National Dis-

aster Interfaith Network and USC Center for Religion and Civic Culture's Field Guide, help enhance their effectiveness.

These responses highlight the pivotal role that faith communities can play in providing for the needs of society amid a crisis. Faith communities, such as churches, mosques, synagogues, and temples, have historically been at the forefront of relief efforts during times of crisis. They have the unique ability to mobilize their members and resources quickly, creating a robust support system for those affected by the crisis. Faith communities often have established networks and partnerships with local organizations and government agencies, allowing them to coordinate efforts and maximize their impact.

Besides providing immediate aid, such as food, shelter, and medical help, faith communities also offer emotional and spiritual support to individuals and families in distress. This holistic approach to crisis response helps to address both the immediate physical needs and the long-term well-being of the community. Faith communities often have a deep-rooted sense of social justice and compassion, which drives them to advocate for systemic change and policy reforms to prevent future crises. Overall, the involvement of faith communities in crisis response is invaluable, as they bring together their unique strengths, values, and resources to provide comprehensive support to those in need.

Modern-Day Crises:

Let us examine current events to see how the church is responding.

Natural disasters: Natural disasters have become increasingly frequent and devastating in recent years, affecting communities all over the world. The church, as a source of hope and support, has been actively responding to these crises. Faced with hurricanes, earthquakes, wildfires, and floods, churches have opened their doors to provide shelter and food for those displaced by the disasters. They have mobilized volunteers to assist in relief efforts, distributing supplies and offering emotional support to those affected. Churches have organized prayer vigils and services to bring comfort and unity to the affected communities. Through these actions, the church has showed its commitment to compassion and aiding those in need during times of natural disasters.

I led three separate mission teams to New Orleans following Hurricane Katrina and can attest to the incredible efforts of churches from across the United States during that time. The devastation was unimaginable, resembling a third-world country in its aftermath.

Our first team arrived just one week after the disaster struck, and the sight that greeted us was overwhelming. There was so much work to be done, and it seemed like the entire city was in disarray. Our team found solace in the only open restaurant in New Orleans proper, a Popeye's chicken barn, where we would gather each day for nourishment.

As for accommodation, we were fortunate enough to be allowed to stay in a local church, where we slept in the Sunday School rooms and used their kitchen to cook our meals. For ten days, we dedicated ourselves to the arduous task of mucking out the mud and silt that the storm surge had mercilessly deposited inside people's homes.

Throughout our time there, the church was palpable, providing support and help even when government aid was scarce. To protect ourselves from the bacteria-laden environment, we donned the flimsy white paper suits provided by FEMA, along with face masks. One particularly harrowing experience involved crossing Lake Pontchartrain on portable pontoon bridge sections. The ride was nerve-wracking, to say the least. These experiences taught me the power of unity and compassion in the face of adversity, as churches from across the nation came together to lend a helping hand to the people of New Orleans in their time of need.

Pandemics: Pandemics are global outbreaks of infectious diseases that spread rapidly and affect numerous people across different countries or continents. These outbreaks can have significant social, economic, and health effects, often leading to widespread illness, loss of life, and disruption of daily life. Various pathogens, such as viruses or bacteria, can cause pandemics, and can arise from both animal-to-human transmission (zoonotic diseases) or human-to-human transmission.

Examples of pandemics in history include the 1918 influenza pandemic, the HIV/AIDS pandemic, and the ongoing COVID-19 pandemic. Governments, healthcare systems, and international organizations respond to pandemics by implementing various control measures, such as quarantine, travel restrictions, social distancing, and vaccination campaigns. Researchers and developers are conducting efforts to find effective treatments and develop vaccines to prevent future pandemics.

The role of Faith in such pandemics includes providing a source of hope and comfort for individuals and communities. During times of crisis, faith can serve as a guiding force, offering solace and strength to those who are struggling. It can offer a sense of purpose and meaning, helping people navigate the uncertainties and challenges that arise during a pandemic.

Faith communities also play a crucial role in providing support and help to those in need, whether it be through organizing relief efforts, offering emotional support, or providing resources and services to vulnerable populations. Faith can foster resilience and unity, bringing people together for a collective response to pandemic challenges. It can promote empathy and compassion, encouraging individuals to look out for one another and prioritize the well-being of the community. Faith can also provide a framework for processing and making sense of the events unfolding, offering guidance on how to navigate ethical dilemmas and make decisions that align with one's values. Overall, faith can play a vital role in helping individuals and communities cope with the physical, emotional, and spiritual effects of a pandemic.

I have friends who have volunteered from their respective churches at our local hospital to do such menial tasks as handing out masks, giving directions to health care, and providing information to help during their recovery. These are angels in masks who show the love of God in everything they do.

Economic Hardships: Economic hardships are a pervasive issue that affects numerous communities worldwide. These challenges can arise from various factors, including unemployment, poverty, inflation, and economic recessions. When faced with such difficulties, faith-driven responses have emerged as powerful forces of resilience and support.

These responses often originate from religious institutions, such as churches, mosques, temples, and synagogues, which play a crucial role in providing aid and help to those in need. Faith-based organizations and individuals offer a wide range of services, including food banks, shelters, financial help programs, job training, and counseling, to help ease the economic burdens faced by vulnerable populations.

These faith-driven responses go beyond material support, as they also provide a sense of community, hope, and spiritual guidance to individuals grappling with economic hardships. In this document, we will delve into the specific communities affected by economic hardships and explore the remarkable faith-driven responses that have emerged as beacons of hope in the face of adversity.

The Role of Prayer and Worship:

Prayer is a spiritual practice that holds immense significance in various religious traditions across the world. It is communication with a higher power or divine entity where individuals express their thoughts, feelings, and desires. Prayer serves to seek guidance, offering gratitude, seeking forgiveness, and finding solace and strength in times of difficulty. People often view prayer as establishing a connection with the divine and aligning themselves with a greater purpose or higher power.

Prayer can take various forms, including recitation of sacred texts, silent meditation, chanting, or communal gatherings. Many believe prayer has the power to bring about positive changes in one's life and to create a sense of peace and inner harmony. The act of prayer can also foster a sense of community and unity among believers as they come together to share their faith and seek collective blessings. In addition, prayer can be a source of comfort and hope, providing individuals with a sense of purpose and reassurance during challenging times. Overall, prayer plays a vital role in the spiritual and emotional well-being of individuals, offering them a means to connect with the divine and find solace, guidance, and strength in their lives.

How do other faith practices (apart from Christianity) provide comfort and resilience during crises?

During times of crisis, individuals turn to their faith practices to find solace and strength. While Christianity is one of the major religions that offers comfort, there are many other faith traditions that also provide support and resilience. For example, **Islam**, one of the world's largest religions, teaches its followers to rely on their faith in Allah during difficult times. **Muslims** find comfort in reciting the Quran, engaging in prayer, and seeking guidance from their imams.

Similarly, **Buddhism** emphasizes mindfulness and meditation to find inner peace and overcome adversity. Buddhists often turn to their teachings, such as the Four Noble Truths and the Eightfold Path, to navigate through crises.

Hinduism, with its diverse practices, encourages adherents to find solace in their devotion to deities and rituals. Hindus may seek guidance from priests, engage in spiritual practices like yoga and meditation, or participate in religious festivals to find comfort and resilience.

Other faith traditions such as **Sikhism**, **Judaism**, and Indigenous religions also have their own unique ways of providing comfort and strength during challenging times. These practices may include reciting scriptures, engaging in communal rituals, seeking guidance from religious leaders, or connecting with nature and ancestral spirits.

Overall, the multitude of faith practices beyond Christianity offer individuals diverse avenues for finding resilience amidst crises.

The Inevitability of Crises in Human Coexistence

Crisis situations are an inherent part of human coexistence. Regardless of the social, cultural, or geographical context, as long as two individuals exist side-by-side, the potential for conflicts and challenges arises. This chapter has explored the reasons behind the perpetual presence of crises in human relationships, shedding light on the complex dynamics that contribute to their occurrence.

1. Diverse Perspectives and Interests:

One of the primary drivers of crises in human coexistence is the diversity of perspectives and interests that individuals bring to any situation. Each person possesses a unique set of values, beliefs, and priorities, which can often clash with those of others. These differences can lead to misunderstandings, disagreements, and ultimately escalate into crises if not effectively addressed through open communication and compromise.

2. Limited Resources and Competition:

Competition arises from the scarcity of global resources. Whether it is access to land, wealth, power, or necessities like food and water, the struggle to secure these resources can give rise to crises. This competition may lead to conflicts, ranging from personal disputes to large-scale societal tensions, as people strive to safeguard their own interests and ensure their survival.

3. Power Struggles and Inequality:

Power dynamics and inequalities often characterize human societies. These imbalances can manifest in various forms, such as economic disparities, political dominance, or social hierarchies. When power becomes concentrated in the hands of a few or when marginalized groups face systemic discrimination, it creates an environment ripe for crises. The oppressed may rise against their oppressors, seeking justice and equality, while those in power may resist relinquishing their authority, leading to prolonged conflicts.

4. Differences in Values and Beliefs:

Human beings hold a wide range of values and beliefs shaped by their upbringing, education, and cultural backgrounds. These differences can cause clashes of ideologies, religious conflicts, or moral dilemmas, all of which have the potential to escalate into crises. Disputes over fundamental principles, such as human rights, social justice, or ethical practices, often ignite passionate debates and struggles for change, further contributing to the perpetuation of crises.

Crises are an inevitable aspect of human coexistence because of the inherent diversity, competition for resources, power struggles, and differences in values and beliefs. While they can be disruptive and challenging, crises also present opportunities for growth, resolution, and the development of stronger relationships. By understanding and addressing the root causes of crises, societies can strive towards fostering greater understanding, empathy, and cooperation, mitigating their impact and creating a more harmonious coexistence.

The Church Responds

Being able to find strength during a crisis is a significant part of the Christian experience. Various communities draw on their faith, personal stories, and biblical teachings to navigate these challenges. This chapter leads us through an examination of such crisis and how the church responds. In times of crisis, Christians often turn to prayer as a source of solace and guidance. They rely on the belief that God is present in their lives and will provide comfort and strength in difficult times.

Personal stories of overcoming adversity can serve as powerful testimonies of hope and resilience for others going through similar struggles. The Bible also offers a wealth of teachings and examples that can inspire and provide wisdom during times of crisis. Verses such as Jeremiah 29:11, which assures believers that God has plans to prosper them and give them hope for the future, can provide reassurance and a sense of purpose.

The church community plays a vital role in providing support and encouragement during times of crisis. Churches often organize prayer vigils, support groups, and outreach programs to assist those in need. They create a space where individuals can come together, share their burdens, and find strength in their shared faith. Overall, a deep reliance on God, the power of personal stories, and the support of the church community marks the Christian experience during a crisis.

Mary was a dedicated member of Long Branch Methodist Church, a tight-knit community church nestled in a quiet town. Despite its small size, the church had a reputation for its immense compassion and unwavering support for its members.

Mary found solace and strength in this community when her husband's devastating diagnosis turned her world upside down. The news of his serious illness shook their lives, leaving them with a sense of fear and uncertainty.

However, Mary soon discovered that she was not alone in her struggle. The church, like a beacon of hope, rallied around her family, extending their love and assistance in every way imaginable. They did not just offer meals or send well wishes; they became an integral part of Mary's support system, embracing her with open arms and providing a shoulder to lean on.

The church community proved to be an unwavering

source of comfort, offering not only practical help but also the power of collective prayer. To aid Dan, Mary's husband, the community held special prayer meetings, lifting his name in prayer and seeking divine intervention. The impact of this collective effort was remarkable, not just for Mary and her family, but for the entire church family.

The bond between the community and the church grew immeasurably stronger during this difficult time, as they witnessed firsthand the transformative power of faith, hope, and unwavering support. Long Branch Methodist Church emerged from this trial as a beacon of resilience and love, forever changed by the journey they embarked on with one of their own.

Dan and Mary, a devoted couple in their church community, faced a challenging ordeal that tested their faith and resilience. Despite the difficulties, they found solace and strength in their shared belief in God's power. The scripture in Philippians 4:13, "I can do all things through Christ who strengthens me," resonated deeply with them during this trying time. It served as a constant reminder that, with God's help, they could overcome any obstacle.

The church community, recognizing their unwavering faith, rallied around them, offering prayers and support throughout the entire journey. After a long and arduous battle, doctors finally diagnosed Dan as cured, answering their prayers. This miraculous turn of events served as a testament to the power of prayer and the unwavering support of a loving community.

Isaiah 41:10 is a powerful verse in the Bible that provides us with the promise of God's unwavering presence and support. In this verse, God assures us of His constant presence, saying, "So do not fear, for I am with you; do not be dismayed, for I am your God. I will strengthen you and help you; I will uphold you with my righteous right hand."

These words serve as a source of comfort and encouragement, reminding us that no matter what challenges or difficulties we may face, God is always by our side, ready to strengthen and guide us. This promise shows God's faithfulness and love towards His people, instilling in us a sense of confidence and reassurance as we navigate through life's trials. It serves as a reminder that we are never alone, and that we can rely on God's unwavering support to overcome any obstacle that comes our way.

It is truly amazing to watch the church **BE** the church! When it rallies around those within or without its walls, the world becomes a better place. When the faithful collaborate for good, things happen. These actions subtly and incrementally change the world.

The group dedicated time to pray for James and his family, providing spiritual support that kept his spirit lifted during this challenging time. The combination of practical assistance, emotional support, and prayers from the church support group played a significant role in James' journey towards overcoming his financial hardship. With their help, James regained hope and resilience, and eventually, he could secure a new job that allowed him to provide for his family and rebuild their lives.

Psalm 23:4 is a powerful verse that serves as a constant reminder of God's unwavering comfort and guidance. It speaks to the resilience and courage we can find in the face of adversity. The verse begins by acknowledging the reality of walking through the darkest valley, a metaphorical representation of the most challenging and difficult times in our lives.

Despite the darkness and uncertainty that may surround us, the verse encourages us to have faith and trust in God, assuring us we need not fear any evil. This statement is a testament to the protective and nurturing presence of

God, who is always by our side. The verse mentions the rod and staff, symbolic tools used by shepherds to guide and protect their flock. In this context, they represent God's constant watchfulness and support. The mention of these instruments brings a sense of comfort, as they serve as a reminder that God is always there to guide us and provide us with the strength we need to face any challenges that come our way. Overall, Psalm 23:4 serves as a source of solace and reassurance, reminding us that even in the darkest of times, we are never alone.

Romans 8:28 serves as an unwavering assurance for believers that God is actively working in every circumstance, regardless of its nature, to bring about good. This powerful statement from the Apostle Paul provides comfort and encouragement to those who place their trust in God's plan. It reminds us that even amid challenging and difficult situations, we can find solace knowing that God is present and actively involved in our lives. This verse serves as a reminder to remain steadfast in our faith and trust in God's sovereignty, knowing that He is orchestrating everything for our ultimate benefit. It is a source of hope and reassurance, reminding us that even when we cannot see the bigger picture, God's plans are always for our good.

"And we know that in all things God works for the good of those who love him, who have been called according to his purpose." (Romans 8:28)

For the Church, let me share at least five ways that we can offer our help and reach out to those in our community who need us.

Prayer and meditation are important spiritual practices that allow individuals to connect with a higher power, such as God. Through prayer, individuals express their thoughts, feelings, and desires to God, seeking comfort, guidance, and strength. It provides a sense of peace and tranquility as individuals feel heard and understood by a divine being.

Meditation involves focusing one's attention and quieting the mind, allowing for a deeper connection with one's inner self and the divine. It helps individuals to cultivate mindfulness, reduce anxiety, and gain clarity in their thoughts and actions. One can practice prayer and meditation individually or in a group, customizing them to one's personal beliefs and religious traditions. Overall, these practices offer a profound and transformative experience, nurturing the spiritual growth and well-being of individuals.

Community Support: Christian communities often come together to support one another, offering practical help, emotional support, and spiritual encouragement. This support can take various forms, such as organizing meals for families in need during times of illness or crisis, providing financial help to those facing financial difficulties, and offering guidance and counseling to individuals struggling with personal issues.

Community members often create a space for open dialogue and sharing, where individuals can express their concerns and receive comfort and understanding from their fellow believers. This sense of belonging and interconnectedness helps foster a strong support system within the community, allowing individuals to lean on one another in times of need.

Christian communities frequently engage in prayer circles and Bible studies, providing spiritual guidance and encouragement to uplift and strengthen each other's faith. These supportive acts provide practical help and emotional comfort, while also fostering a stronger sense of community and unity among believers. Overall, the commitment to community support within Christian communities serves as a testament to the value placed on caring for one another and living out the teachings of Jesus Christ.

Worship and Music: Participating in worship services is a fundamental aspect of religious practice for various believers. It provides an opportunity for individuals to come together as a community and express their devotion and reverence to their faith.

Whether it is through the recitation of prayers, the reading of sacred texts, or the singing of hymns and spiritual songs, worship services serve as a platform for believers to connect with their higher power and seek guidance, solace, and inspiration. Music's power in worship is undeniable. The melodic tunes and harmonious melodies have a profound impact on the spiritual experience, evoking deep emotions and fostering a sense of unity among worshippers.

Whether it is the majestic sound of an organ, the rhythmic beats of drums, or the angelic voices of a choir, the music in worship can uplift and strengthen believers, transcending language barriers and cultural differences. Listening to or singing hymns and spiritual songs outside of worship services can also provide a source of comfort and encouragement on one's personal faith journey. The lyrics often contain profound truths and messages that resonate with believers and remind them of the divine presence in their lives. Therefore, engaging in worship and embracing the power of music can be transformative, deepening one's connection to their faith and nourishing the soul.

Scriptural Study: Studying the Bible and reflecting on its teachings can provide wisdom and reassurance. The Bible is a sacred text that holds deep meaning and guidance for millions of people around the world. Different authors, inspired by God, wrote the various books of the Old and New Testaments over many centuries. Engaging in scriptural study involves reading and analyzing the passages, understanding their historical and cultural contexts, and contemplating their relevance to our lives today.

Through this process, individuals can gain insights into moral and ethical principles, learn about God, and find comfort in times of uncertainty. The Bible offers timeless wisdom and timeless truths that can help individuals navigate the complexities of life and make informed decisions.

Scriptural study often involves prayer and meditation, allowing individuals to deepen their spiritual connection with God and find solace in His teachings. This practice benefits people of various faith traditions, regardless of specific religious denomination or belief system, because they can benefit from the Bible's profound messages. Whether seeking guidance, seeking solace, or seeking a deeper understanding of faith, scriptural study provides a valuable opportunity for personal growth and spiritual nourishment.

Acts of Service: Serving others, whether within the church or the broader community, can help individuals find purpose and strength. Acts of service encompass diverse activities, like volunteering at a local soup kitchen, participating in mission trips, or helping older adult neighbors with chores. These acts not only benefit those being served, but also have a profound impact on the individuals performing the acts.

Engaging in acts of service allows individuals to connect with their community and develop a sense of belonging and purpose. By helping others, individuals often experience a sense of fulfillment and satisfaction, knowing that they are making a positive difference in the lives of others.

Acts of service can also serve as a source of personal growth and self-discovery. They provide opportunities to develop new skills, expand one's perspective, and build empathy and compassion.

The act of serving others can be a transformative experience, as it allows individuals to challenge themselves, step outside their comfort zone, and develop a greater understanding of the world around them.

Ultimately, acts of service not only benefit the recipients but also have the power to transform individuals and communities for the better.

Thus, we ask the underlying question: **where does the church go from here?** How does the church become the true church God expects of his people? In order to answer these questions, we must delve into the current state of the church and identify areas for improvement.

The church can start by focusing on strengthening its spiritual foundation. This involves encouraging members to deepen their relationship with God through prayer, Bible study, and worship. The church should prioritize fostering a sense of community and inclusivity. This means actively reaching out to marginalized groups, embracing diversity, and creating a safe space for everyone to worship and participate. The church must actively engage in social justice issues and take a stand against inequality, discrimination, and injustice. By advocating for the voiceless and being a force for positive change, the church can truly embody the values that God expects for his people.

Finally, the church should develop and train its leaders, ensuring they possess the skills and knowledge to guide and serve the congregation. By implementing these strategies, the church can evolve into an accurate reflection of God's love and teachings, creating a powerful impact on the lives of its members and the world around them. Pastoral leadership is a key ingredient to this creative work.

We now turn our attention to **Case Studies of Global Crises and the Church's Response.**

If we are to be "the Church," a collective body of believers, it is imperative that we show proactivity and compassion when confronted with global crises occurring in different parts of the world. It is not enough to remain ignorant or indifferent, akin to a bird with its head buried in the sand. Instead, we must actively engage with the issues at hand, seeking to understand the root causes and effects of these crises.

By doing so, we can effectively respond and provide support to those affected, both through prayer and tangible acts of help. As members of the Church, it is our responsibility to extend love, empathy, and resources to those in need, regardless of their geographical location. This requires us to stay informed about global events, mobilize resources, and collaborate with organizations and individuals working towards alleviating the suffering caused by these crises. Together, we can make a meaningful and lasting impact, embodying the principles of compassion, justice, and solidarity that define our faith.

There are many crises in the world today. For instance, one of the most pressing crises is the ongoing global pandemic caused by the spread of the novel coronavirus, **COVID-19**. This crisis has resulted in significant health, economic, and social challenges across the globe. The pandemic has overwhelmed healthcare systems, led to countless loss of lives, and triggered a severe economic downturn with widespread job losses and business closures. There is a growing concern over the mental health effects of prolonged isolation and uncertainty. The pandemic has also exposed and exacerbated existing inequalities, with marginalized communities being disproportionately affected.

Another crisis that demands urgent attention is the **climate crisis**. The world is experiencing more frequent and intense natural disasters, such as hurricanes, wildfires, and droughts, which are linked to climate change. These disasters have devastating consequences for ecosystems, livelihoods, and human lives. There is a growing refugee crisis, with millions of people displaced from their homes because of conflicts, violence, and persecution. These displaced individuals face immense hardships, including limited access to necessities such as food, water, and healthcare. These are just a few examples of the crises that the world is currently grappling with, highlighting the urgent need for collective action and solutions.

The Bible's teachings deeply root the church's responsibilities in these global crises. The scriptures provide guidance and instruction on how the church should respond to various challenges and crises that affect humanity on a global scale. From caring for the poor and marginalized to promoting justice and peace, the Bible calls upon the church to be engaged in addressing the needs of the world. It highlights the importance of showing compassion, extending help to those in need, and offering comfort and support to the afflicted.

The Bible emphasizes the significance of unity, encouraging the church to come together as a community to tackle these crises collectively. In times of global turmoil, the church is called to be a beacon of hope, spreading love, compassion, and faith to bring healing and restoration to a hurting world.

Here are a few scripture references to consider:

Matthew 25:35-36 - "For I was hungry, and you gave me something to eat, I was thirsty and you gave me something to drink, I was a stranger and you invited me in, I needed clothes and you clothed me, I was sick and you looked after me, I was in prison and you came to visit me." This passage encourages the church to provide practical help to those in need.

Galatians 6:2 states, "Carry each other's burdens, and in this way you will fulfill the law of Christ."

Isaiah 58:10 - "If you spend yourselves on behalf of the hungry and satisfy the needs of the oppressed, then your light will rise in the darkness, and your night will become like the noonday." This scripture speaks to the act of selfless giving and helping those who are suffering.

James 2:15-16 - "Suppose a brother or a sister is without clothes and daily food. If one of you says to them, 'Go in peace; keep warm and well-fed,' but does nothing about their physical needs, what good is it?" This verse reminds the church of the importance of not only offering words of comfort but also taking concrete actions to help those in need.

Micah 6:8 - "He has shown you, O mortal, what is good. And what does the Lord require of you? To act justly and to love mercy and to walk humbly with your God." This verse calls on the church to pursue justice, love mercy, and walk humbly, reflecting God's character in their response to crises.

While the wars and pandemics continue to devastate communities and economies globally, it is crucial for our church to maintain a vigilant and compassionate stance. In these challenging times, it is our duty to seek opportunities actively to provide relief and support to those in need. By harnessing our collective resources and mobilizing our congregation, we can make a meaningful impact on the lives of individuals and communities affected by these crises.

Through various initiatives such as fundraising, volunteering, and collaborating with local organizations, we can extend a helping hand to those who are suffering and bring hope to their lives. Together, as a united church, we have the power to make a difference amid these ongoing challenges.

In my church, The United Methodist Church, we have

established The Board of Global Ministries as the outreach arm of the church. The Board of Global Ministries is a vital component of our church's mission to serve and support communities around the world. This board coordinates and implements various initiatives and programs that aim to address global issues such as poverty, hunger, healthcare, education, and social justice. In collaboration with local churches, organizations, and individuals, the Board of Global Ministries works to affect sustainable, transformative community change globally.

By providing resources, funding, and volunteers, we actively engage in projects that promote peace, equality, and love for our neighbors. Our church firmly believes in the importance of spreading the teachings of Jesus Christ through acts of service and compassion, and the Board of Global Ministries plays a crucial role in fulfilling this mission. Together, we work towards building a more just, inclusive, and compassionate world, one community at a time.

The Catholic Church, being a global institution, recognizes the importance of addressing and responding to global crises. In order to extend its support and aid to those affected by such crises, the Church has established an extensive outreach program. This program encompasses various initiatives and projects aimed at providing assistance and relief to communities facing challenges such as natural disasters, conflict, poverty, and health epidemics. Through partnerships with local organizations, the Catholic Church mobilizes resources and volunteers to offer immediate relief efforts, including emergency supplies, medical assistance, and shelter.

The Church focuses on long-term solutions by investing in sustainable development projects, education, and capacity building programs. This comprehensive outreach program reflects the Church's commitment to serving and empowering those in need, irrespective of their geographical location, race, or religion.

There are many outreach programs in local churches of different denominations who are responding in our global crisis as well. Among these are food pantries and soup kitchens that provide meals for individuals and families facing food insecurity. These programs often rely on donations from community members and volunteers to support their efforts.

Many churches are offering financial help to those struggling to pay bills or facing job loss because of the pandemic. They provide support through emergency funds and financial counseling services. Some churches are collaborating with local organizations to provide shelter and resources for individuals experiencing homelessness, ensuring they have a safe place to stay during these challenging times. These outreach programs play a vital role in addressing the needs of vulnerable populations and fostering a sense of community support and resilience in the face of adversity.

When **Hurricane Katrina** hit the New Orleans area on August 29, 2005, the church I pastored, Sylvania First UMC, immediately mobilized to provide aid and support to the affected communities. Recognizing the urgent need for assistance, we quickly organized two crews of dedicated volunteers, totaling 20 individuals, and loaded up our church van with essential tools and supplies. We equipped our team with chainsaws, hammers, emergency kits, and a firm determination to serve those affected by the devastating hurricane.

Upon arriving in New Orleans, a local church graciously offered us lodging in their Sunday School rooms, which became our temporary base of operations. The resilience and hospitality of the community were evident as we settled in and prepared ourselves for the challenging work ahead. Cooking our meals in the church kitchen, we not only sustained ourselves, but also fostered a sense of unity and camaraderie among the team.

A haunting and somber sight met us as we ventured into the once vibrant and bustling heart of New Orleans. The streets were eerily empty, devoid of the usual hustle and bustle of daily life. The devastation left in the wake of Hurricane Katrina was staggering, with buildings damaged, debris scattered, and a palpable sense of loss hanging in the air.

Undeterred by the desolation, our church crew remained steadfast in our mission to assist in the clean-up and recovery efforts. We tirelessly worked to clear fallen trees, remove debris, and repair damaged structures, doing our utmost to restore a sense of normalcy to the shattered lives of those affected. The days were long and physically demanding, but the gratitude and resilience of the people we encountered fueled our determination to continue making a difference.

Our time in New Orleans during those post-Katrina days was a profound experience that left an indelible mark on our hearts. The devastation we witnessed was heartbreaking, but the opportunity to serve and support those in need reminded us of the power of unity and compassion. The church's response to the disaster exemplified the true spirit of community, as we joined hands with countless others to rebuild, restore, and bring hope to a city in desperate need.

This is how the church responds to crises. We must be pro-active and reach out to the less-fortunate among us and do the work of the gospel of Christ.

I am now retired and attend First United Methodist Church in Statesboro, Georgia. Our church is a vibrant and welcoming community of believers. One highlight of our church is the incredible soup kitchen that we have. Every week, dedicated volunteers come together to serve hot meals to those in need in our local area. It is truly heartwarming to see the impact we make in the lives of so many individuals by providing them with not just a nourishing meal, but also a sense of belonging and fellowship.

Besides our soup kitchen, First United Methodist Church deeply commits itself to missions and global ministries. We believe it is our duty as followers of Christ to spread love and compassion beyond our immediate community. Through our various mission initiatives, we actively support and contribute to projects that aim to improve the lives of people in different parts of the world. Our church dedicates itself to positively affecting the lives of others by providing clean water, medical aid, education, and disaster relief.

As a member of the First United Methodist Church, I am proud to be part of a congregation that prioritizes missions. In fact, I firmly believe that a church should not exist solely for the sake of its own members, but should extend its reach and impact to those who are less fortunate. It is through our commitment to missions that we truly live out the teachings of Jesus Christ, who commanded us to love our neighbors as ourselves.

During the holiday season, our church organized two beautiful Christmas Eve services. These services were not only a time of celebration and worship, but also an opportunity to give back to the community. We took special offerings at both services, with the proceeds going towards supporting the ongoing efforts of our soup kitchen. It was incredibly heartwarming to witness the generosity of our congregation as they opened their hearts and wallets to help those in need.

In conclusion, the First United Methodist Church in

Statesboro, Georgia, is a church that is actively involved in making a positive impact in our community and beyond. Our soup kitchen serves as a beacon of hope for those facing food insecurity, while our commitment to missions allows us to extend our reach and bring about a change in the lives of people around the world. I am grateful to be part of such a caring and compassionate church family, where we put our faith into action and strive to be the hands and feet of Jesus.

2

Persecution and Modern-Day Martyrs

A MARTYR IS SOMEONE who suffers death because of their religious beliefs, often as a testimony to their faith. People most commonly associate the term with individuals killed for refusing to renounce their religion or beliefs under persecution or oppressive regimes. Many religions include the concept of martyrdom; these religions venerate martyrs for their unwavering devotion and sacrifice. Their stories often serve as powerful symbols of faith and courage for others in the community. Remember: there are no living martyrs.

Christians often honor and remember martyrs for their ultimate sacrifice in the face of persecution. People celebrate early Christian martyrs such as Stephen, Peter, and Paul, and countless others throughout history, for their unwavering faith and their willingness to suffer and die for their beliefs.

This chapter will delve into the lives of several remarkable individuals who became martyrs because of their unwavering faith in Christ and their commitment to their personal beliefs. Through their inspiring stories, we will gain insight into the immense hardships and persecutions they endured. These brave souls faced unimaginable challenges, ranging from imprisonment and torture to public ridicule and ostracization.

Despite the immense pressures and threats they faced, these martyrs remained steadfast in their devotion to Christ and refused to renounce their beliefs. Through their unwavering commitment and sacrifice, they became shining examples of courage, resilience, and unwavering faith. In exploring their lives, we will not only honor their memory but also draw valuable lessons and inspiration from their extraordinary journey.

Old Testament

We begin with Old Testament martyrs. The Bible, in Genesis 4:8, recounts how Cain brutally murdered Abel out of jealousy, making Abel the first martyr. God accepted only Abel's offering after both brothers had made offerings to Him, resulting in this tragedy. This enraged Cain, leading him to commit the unthinkable act of taking his brother's life.

Abel's unwavering faith and righteousness, even in the face of persecution, established him as a symbol of martyrdom in the early biblical narratives. His story serves as a testament to the sacrifices made by those who choose to stand firm in their beliefs, even in the face of extreme adversity.

In Genesis 37:28, we encounter the story of **Joseph**, a significant figure in biblical history. Joseph, the second martyr, faced a tragic fate as his own brothers ruthlessly sold into slavery him. This act of betrayal marked a turning point in Joseph's life, propelling him into a series of remarkable events and ultimately shaping the destiny of the Israelite nation.

Despite the hardships he endured, Joseph's unwavering faith and resilience serve as an inspiration to generations of believers. His incredible journey from slavery to becoming a trusted advisor to Pharaoh, the ruler of Egypt, showcases the power of divine providence and the triumph of righteousness. This pivotal moment in Joseph's life sets the stage for a captivating narrative that unfolds with themes of forgiveness, redemption, and divine intervention.

Moses, the central figure in the biblical narrative of Exodus, encountered formidable opposition throughout his journey. In Exodus 2:15, we witness Moses escaping Egypt after killing an Egyptian who was mistreating an Israelite slave. However, resistance and skepticism greeted Moses when he returned to his people. His own people questioned his intentions and authority, making his mission to liberate them from slavery an arduous task.

Pharaoh, the ruler of Egypt, proved to be a relentless adversary for Moses. In Numbers 14:1-10, we observe the Israelites' lack of faith in God's promise to deliver them to the Promised Land. The fearful report of the spies who had explored the land fueled their doubts. As a result, they rebelled against Moses, expressing their desire to return to Egypt. This rebellion reached its peak when the Israelites even contemplated stoning Moses and Aaron, demonstrating the extent of their opposition to their leaders.

In both instances, Moses faced considerable challenges from both the ruling authority and his own people. Despite these obstacles, Moses persevered with unwavering determination, relying on his faith in God's guidance to lead the Israelites towards their liberation and eventual journey to the land flowing with milk and honey. His story stands as a testament to the resilience and strength required to overcome opposition in the pursuit of a greater cause.

David, a young and talented shepherd, found himself in a precarious situation as King Saul relentlessly pursued him. The biblical account of 1 Samuel 19:1-2 tells this gripping tale. Because of David's remarkable success in battle and his growing popularity among the people, Saul's jealousy and fear consumed him. In his paranoid state, the king sought to eliminate the perceived threat that David posed for his reign.

Determined to take David's life, Saul mobilized his forces and pursued the young shepherd throughout the vast and treacherous landscapes of ancient Israel. Despite the constant threat to his life, David displayed unwavering courage and resourcefulness, finding refuge in the wilderness and seeking the guidance of the Lord. This thrilling narrative depicts the timeless struggle between power and righteousness; The relentless pursuit of an envious and insecure king tests David's unwavering faith and resilience.

They imprisoned **Jeremiah**, the Lord's prophet, and threw him into a cistern, putting him in a dire situation.

Jeremiah 38:6 records this incident, highlighting the challenges Jeremiah faced for faithfully delivering God's messages to the people of Judah. A deep, narrow water pit, the cistern served as his makeshift prison, symbolizing the depths of Jeremiah's despair.

It is important to note that this was not the first time he faced persecution for proclaiming God's word, as his unwavering commitment often clashed with the political and religious leaders of his time. Despite the darkness and isolation of the cistern, Jeremiah's faith remained steadfast, providing a powerful testimony of resilience and trust in God, even in the most challenging circumstances.

A precarious situation arose for **Daniel**, a faithful servant of God, when someone threw him into the lions' den. This harrowing event unfolded because of his unwavering devotion to his beliefs. According to the biblical account in Daniel 6:16, Daniel's adversaries plotted against him because of jealousy and envy. These individuals, driven by their own malicious intentions, conspired to bring Daniel down by exploiting his faith.

They convinced King Darius to issue a decree that prohibited anyone from praying to any god or human except the king himself. However, Daniel remained steadfast in his commitment to God and continued to pray three times a day, openly defying the king's decree. Faced with this blatant act of disobedience, Daniel's adversaries seized the opportunity to accuse him before the king, who reluctantly ordered his faithful servant to be cast into the den of hungry lions. It is within this context that we witness Daniel's incredible display of faith and trust in God's protection as he willingly faced the ferocious beasts.

New Testament

The New Testament is a collection of religious texts that documents the life and teachings of Jesus Christ and the early Christian community. Within its pages, there are numerous accounts of martyrdom, a solemn and impactful theme that shapes the narrative.

One such example is the story of **John the Baptist**, a prominent figure who played a crucial role in preparing the way for Jesus. The Gospel of Matthew recounts King Herod's tragic beheading of John the Baptist. Matthew 14:10 describes this event, underscoring the challenges and sacrifices faced by those who dedicated themselves to spreading the message of Christianity. The New Testament's inclusion of martyrdom stories serves to inspire and commemorate the steadfast faith and dedication of individuals who will lay down their lives for their beliefs.

A mob brutally stoned **Stephen**, a Christian disciple, to death for his unwavering commitment to his beliefs. The passage in Acts 7:54-60 vividly depicts the persecution of early Christians and records this tragic incident. Stephen's unwavering faith and bold proclamation of the Gospel challenged the religious authorities of his time, leading to a violent reaction from the crowd.

As the stones hurled towards him, Stephen, filled with the Holy Spirit, looked up to heaven and saw the glory of God. Despite the excruciating pain and imminent death, he forgave his attackers and prayed for their forgiveness. This act of mercy and love showcased Stephen's exceptional character and unwavering commitment to his faith. Stephen's martyrdom not only serves as a testament to his unwavering conviction but also highlights the immense sacrifices made by early Christians in spreading the message of Christianity.

James, who was the brother of John and one of the twelve apostles, tragically met his untimely demise at the hands of Herod, the ruler of Judea. It was under Herod's oppressive reign that he issued the fateful order for James to be executed by the sword. The book of Acts, specifically Acts 12:2, records this brutal act of violence against a prominent early Christian.

His brother John and the rest of the disciples deeply felt the loss of James, mourning their beloved companion and dedicated servant of the faith. This tragic event serves as a somber reminder of the challenges faced by the early followers of Jesus and the persecution they endured for their unwavering commitment to spreading the gospel message.

Authorities arrested **Peter and John**, two prominent apostles of Jesus Christ, and threw them into prison for their unwavering commitment to spreading their Lord's teachings. This incident occurred in the early days of the formation of the early Christian community.

The religious authorities, threatened by the growing influence of these fearless messengers, sought to silence them through imprisonment and physical punishment. Not only were Peter and John deprived of their freedom, but they also endured brutal beatings at the hands of their captors. Despite the immense physical and emotional pain they experienced, their faith remained unshaken.

The Book of Acts, specifically Acts 5:40, records this event, attesting to the unwavering dedication of these apostles and their enduring commitment to spreading the message of love, forgiveness, and salvation.

The apostle **Paul**, a prominent figure in early Christianity, faced immense persecution and hardship throughout his life. Despite his unwavering dedication to spreading the teachings of Jesus Christ, opposition and hostility met Paul's efforts. Notably, Paul experienced imprisonment, physical abuse, and ultimately met his demise through execution. In 2 Corinthians 11:23-28, Paul details his numerous imprisonments, floggings, and exposures to dangers. This passage serves as a testament to Paul's resilience and unwavering commitment to his faith, even in the face of immense adversity.

In 2 Timothy 4:6-8, Paul acknowledges his imminent death, expressing his readiness to face the final judgment. Despite the hardships he endured, Paul's unwavering faith and determination to fulfill his mission remained unshaken, leaving behind a powerful legacy that continues to inspire and guide Christians around the world.

The apostle **John**, one of the twelve disciples of Jesus Christ, faced a period of exile during his old age. Revelation 1:9 tells us that someone exiled John to the island of Patmos. Patmos is a small Greek island in the Aegean

Sea, known for its rugged landscapes and serene beauty. They exiled John to Patmos because of his unwavering commitment to spreading the teachings of Jesus Christ.

During his time on the island, John received a series of divine revelations, which he later recorded in the book of Revelation. These revelations provided insights into the future events and the ultimate triumph of good over evil. Despite the hardships of exile, John's time in Patmos became a significant period of spiritual enlightenment and contributed to the rich tapestry of biblical literature.

Around the World

You can find martyrs, individuals who sacrificed their lives for a cause or belief, in various places around the world. From ancient times to the present day, these courageous individuals have emerged in different cultures and regions, leaving their mark on history.

Some martyrs are associated with religious movements, such as the early Christian martyrs who faced persecution for their faith. Political struggles link others, such as activists who fought for civil rights and freedom in various countries.

Social movements also include martyrs; individuals in these movements have sacrificed their lives. No matter the setting, martyrs serve as symbols of bravery, resilience, and unwavering commitment to their cause, inspiring generations to come.

In **Nigeria**, the extremist group known as Boko Haram has conducted a series of violent attacks targeting Christians, resulting in the brutal slaughter of over 10,000 individuals. In 2002, founders established Boko Haram, meaning "Western education is forbidden," which has since perpetrated numerous acts of terrorism and insurgency in the country. The group's primary aim is to establish an Islamic state in Nigeria and eradicate any form of Western influence, particularly Christianity.

Boko Haram's relentless campaign of violence has not only claimed the lives of thousands of innocent Christians, but has also caused widespread displacement and destruction of communities. The Nigerian government, along with international organizations and neighboring countries, has been engaged in efforts to combat and dismantle this extremist organization in order to restore peace and security to the affected regions. However, the ongoing threat posed by Boko Haram continues to pose significant challenges for the Nigerian authorities and the global community in their quest for lasting peace and stability.

In **China**, the government has recently escalated its efforts to suppress the practice of Christianity. As part of this crackdown, the government not only blocked Bible apps and Christian websites, but also uses surveillance technology to monitor and control Christian activities. This intrusive surveillance apparatus has created a climate of fear and intimidation, as Christians know constantly that their every move is being watched.

The consequences for openly practicing their faith have become dire, with numerous individuals being arrested and detained simply for their religious beliefs. This oppressive environment has forced many churches to operate covertly, gathering in secret locations to worship and pray. The government's heavy-handed approach to Christianity in China has not only stifled religious freedom, but it has also had a profound impact on the lives of countless believers, who must now navigate a precarious path between their faith and the ever-present threat of persecution.

India has witnessed a disturbing rise in violent attacks targeting Christians by Hindu extremists in recent years. These attacks, often fueled by religious intolerance and bigotry, have resulted in the loss of innocent lives and severe damage to places of worship and Christian communities. Unfortunately, there have been allegations that the Indian government has turned a blind eye to these incidents, failing to take adequate measures to protect the rights and safety of the Christian minority. This has led to growing concerns about the lack of accountability and justice for the victims, exacerbating the sense of vulnerability and fear within the Christian community.

In **Southeast Asia**, Christians face severe persecution from religious extremists. These extremists target and oppress Christians in countries such as Brunei, Laos, the Maldives, Malaysia, Myanmar, and Indonesia. Religious extremists subject Christians in these regions to various forms of discrimination and violence. The denial of basic rights, including religious freedom and freedom of expression, is frequent.

Christians in these countries live in fear and are constantly under threat, as religious extremists actively seek to suppress and eradicate their faith. This persecution forced many to flee their homes or convert, significantly declining the Christian population in these areas. The international community must take notice of this alarming situation and work towards protecting the rights and safety of Christians in Southeast Asia.

Authorities persecute Christians in places like Russia and Ukraine, where authorities suppress religious freedom, and Christians face increasing discrimination and violence. In Russia, for example, the government has implemented strict laws and regulations that severely restrict religious activities, leading to the closure of churches and the arrest of pastors and believers.

Similarly, in Ukraine, conflicts and political tensions have resulted in the targeting of Christians, particularly those who are supporting opposing factions. These believers often face threats, intimidation, and physical harm simply for professing their faith in Jesus Christ. Their stories are heartbreaking and serve as a stark reminder that persecution is a harsh reality for Christians today, regardless of their location or background. It is a global issue that demands attention and action to protect the rights and well-being of those who face such injustice and oppression.

You may ask, "What can I do here in the United States to help relieve persecution and martyrdom in foreign countries?" There are several ways you can contribute to this cause.

To begin, you can educate yourself about the human

rights situation in different countries and stay informed about ongoing conflicts and persecution. This will effectively enable you to advocate for the rights of those affected.

You can support organizations that work towards promoting religious freedom and protecting persecuted individuals and communities. Donating to these organizations or volunteering your time and skills can make a significant impact.

Another important step is to engage in advocacy and raise awareness about the issue. You can write to elected officials, take part in peaceful protests, or use social media to share stories and amplify the voices of the oppressed.

You can encourage dialogue and promote understanding between different communities by actively taking part in interfaith and multicultural events. By fostering empathy and solidarity, you can help build a more inclusive and tolerant society.

Finally, you can support refugees and asylum seekers who have escaped persecution by providing them with assistance, such as language classes, job training, or emotional support. Overall, there are many ways you can contribute to relieving persecution and martyrdom in foreign countries, and it is crucial to take action and advocate for the rights and dignity of all individuals, regardless of their nationality or beliefs.

I was wondering where you will become involved today.

(For further study: www.globalchristianrelief.org; www.persecution.org; and www.thechristianpost.com.)

3

Environmental Stewardship

C HRISTIAN THEOLOGY OFTEN ROOTS the call to care for creation in the belief that God entrusted humanity with Earth's stewardship. This idea is based on several biblical passages, most notably from the book of Genesis. Christians believe that taking care of the environment is a way of honoring God's creation and fulfilling their role as stewards of the Earth.

Key Concepts in the Christian Call to Care for Creation:

Stewardship: Humanity has the responsibility to manage and care for the Earth. As inhabitants of this planet, it is our duty to act as responsible stewards and ensure the well-being and sustainability of the Earth's resources and ecosystems. This entails adopting practices that minimize our negative impact on the environment, such as reducing waste, conserving energy, and protecting biodiversity. It involves making conscious choices in our daily lives to promote a greener and more sustainable future. By practicing stewardship, we can preserve the Earth's natural beauty and resources for future generations to enjoy.

Respect for Creation: All of creation, including the vast expanse of the universe, the intricate ecosystems on Earth, and every living being, is inherently valuable because God makes it. This understanding roots in the belief that God, as the ultimate creator, imbued every aspect of creation with purpose and meaning. From the smallest microorganism to the grandest celestial body, each element of creation reflects the divine wisdom and beauty.

It is our responsibility as human beings to recognize and honor the inherent worth of everything that God has created. This includes not only showing respect towards the natural world but also extending compassion and care towards all living creatures, as they, too, are part of God's intricate design. By cultivating a deep reverence for creation, we can foster a sense of connectedness with the world, leading to a more harmonious and sustainable existence for all.

Sustainability: The church encourages Christians to

use resources to ensure future generations can also enjoy and benefit from them. This principle stems from the belief that God has entrusted humans with the stewardship of the Earth and its resources.

Christians are called to care for creation actively and to be responsible stewards of the environment. This includes practicing sustainable living by reducing waste, conserving energy, and preserving biodiversity.

Christians encourage support for sustainability initiatives, including renewable energy and conservation efforts. By adopting sustainable practices, Christians strive to honor God's creation and leave a positive impact on future generations.

Justice: Environmental care is often linked to social justice, recognizing that environmental degradation disproportionately affects the poor and marginalized. This connection stems from the understanding that marginalized communities have limited access to resources and live in areas with higher levels of pollution and environmental hazards.

These communities often lack the financial means to mitigate the negative impacts of environmental degradation, such as air and water pollution, deforestation, and climate change. They endure the health and economic consequences associated with environmental damage.

Environmental justice advocates argue that addressing these disparities is not only a matter of fairness, but also crucial for achieving a more fair society. By ensuring that all individuals, regardless of their socioeconomic status or background, have equal access to clean air, water, and healthy environments, we can address the systemic inequalities that perpetuate poverty and social injustice.

Racial justice and gender equality, among other forms of social justice, are closely linked to environmental justice. Studies show that environmental degradation disproportionately affects minority and indigenous communities because these communities are more likely to live near industrial facilities and toxic waste sites. Similarly, women in many developing countries must gather water and fuel, which becomes increasingly challenging in areas where natural resources are scarce or polluted.

Considering these interconnected issues, the pursuit of environmental care is not only an environmental imperative but also a moral and ethical responsibility. It requires addressing the root causes of environmental injustice, challenging unsustainable practices, and advocating for policies and practices that prioritize the well-being of all individuals and communities. By doing so, we can build a more just and sustainable future for everyone.

Bible Verses:

The biblical passages of **Genesis 1:28** and **Psalm 24:1** reveal God's divine plan for humanity's responsibility towards the earth and all its inhabitants. These verses emphasize the importance of stewardship, urging humankind to take care of the natural world and its living creatures. In this document, we will delve deeper into the significance of these scriptures, exploring the call to be fruitful, multiply, and govern the earth, while acknowledging God's ultimate ownership and authority over all creation.

Genesis 1:28 - The Blessing of Fruitfulness and Dominion:

In the book of Genesis, God blesses Adam and Eve, the first humans, and instructs them to be fruitful and increase in number. This divine commandment encompasses both physical reproduction and the propagation of humanity. Populating the earth gives humans the opportunity to cultivate and develop a thriving society that reflects God's love and glory.

God grants humanity the authority to "subdue" the

earth and "rule over" the fish, birds, and every living creature. This dominion calls for wise stewardship, not tyrannical or exploitative practices. It is an invitation to manage responsibly the natural resources and ecosystems that sustain life and to care for them. In fulfilling this mandate, humans are called to preserve the harmonious balance of creation, ensuring its wellbeing and flourishing.

Psalm 24:1 - Recognizing God's Sovereignty:

Psalm 24:1 serves as a reminder that despite being given the responsibility to care for the earth, humanity is ultimately accountable to God. It proclaims that the entirety of creation, including the world and all who dwell in it, belongs to the Lord. This verse asserts the divine ownership and sovereignty over all aspects of existence.

Humans are called to approach their stewardship role with humility, reverence, and gratitude, acknowledging that they are mere custodians entrusted with God's creation.

The combination of Genesis 1:28 and Psalm 24:1 establishes a profound theological framework for humanity's relationship with the earth. It emphasizes the dual role of fruitful multiplication and responsible dominion. As stewards of God's creation, humans are called to engage actively in nurturing and protecting the environment, fostering sustainable practices, and ensuring the welfare of all living beings. Simultaneously, they must recognize and respect God's ultimate ownership and authority, humbly submitting to His divine will. By embracing this biblical mandate, humanity can strive towards a harmonious co-existence with nature, honoring God's design for creation.

- **Romans 8:21-22** in the New Testament speaks of a future liberation of creation from its current state of decay and bondage. The passage highlights God bringing creation into the freedom and glory enjoyed by God's children. This passage suggests that the entire creation, including all living beings and the natural world, has been groaning and experiencing the pains of childbirth.

This imagery portrays the present state of creation as one of longing and anticipation for a future transformation. The verse shows that this groaning has been ongoing until the present time, emphasizing the enduring nature of this yearning for liberation.

By highlighting the connection between the liberation of creation and the glory of the children of God, the passage suggests a profound interconnectedness between humanity and the natural world. The passage states that humanity's spiritual journey and ultimate redemption are intricately bound to the fate and flourishing of creation.

Modern Movements:

Many Christian communities have embraced environmental activism, forming organizations and initiatives focused on promoting sustainable practices, conservation, and raising awareness about climate change. By caring for creation, Christians are not only preserving the environment but also loving their neighbors and future generations.

Caring for creation in your daily life can be both rewarding and impactful. Here are some practical steps you can take:

Daily Practices:

1. **Reduce, Reuse, Recycle**: Make recycling a habit, and try to minimize waste by reusing items.

2. **Conserve Energy**: Turn off lights and appliances when not in use, use energy-efficient bulbs, and consider investing in renewable energy sources like solar panels.

3. **Save Water**: Fix leaks, take shorter showers, and use water-saving fixtures.

4. **Eat Sustainably**: Support local farmers, eat more plant-based meals, and reduce food waste.

5. **Reduce Plastic Use**: Use reusable bags, bottles, and containers instead of single-use plastics.

Transportation:

- **Walk or Bike**: Opt for walking or biking instead of driving.

- **Public Transport**: Use public transportation to reduce your carbon footprint.

- **Carpool**: Share rides with others to reduce emissions.

Gardening and Landscaping:

- **Plant Trees**: Trees absorb carbon dioxide and provide oxygen, improving air quality.

- **Native Plants**: Use native plants in your garden that require less water and maintenance.

- **Composting**: Start composting organic waste to enrich the soil and reduce landfill waste.

Consumer Choices:

- **Buy Eco-Friendly Products**: Choose products made from sustainable materials and support companies with green practices.

- **Reduce Meat Consumption**: The meat industry has a significant environmental impact. Reducing meat intake can help lower your ecological footprint.

- **Second-Hand Shopping:** Shopping second-hand reduces the demand for new products and decreases waste.

Get Involved:

- **Volunteer**: Join local environmental groups or initiatives.

- **Educate Others**: Share knowledge about caring for creation with family and friends.

- **Advocate**: Support policies and initiatives that

protect the environment.

Starting small and making gradual changes can lead to a more sustainable and environmentally friendly lifestyle. Every little effort counts in the grand scheme of protecting and preserving our planet.

Meet Sarah, a passionate and environmentally conscious New Yorker who has turned her once barren rooftop into a breathtaking garden oasis. With dedication and a love for nature, Sarah has successfully transformed her urban rooftop into a lush green space that not only brings joy to her life but also contributes positively to the environment.

Sarah's journey began with a few potted plants that she carefully nurtured, and soon enough, her passion for gardening grew. Expanding her repertoire, she took on the challenge of growing her own vegetables, herbs, and flowers. With careful planning and research, Sarah successfully created a diverse and thriving garden that not only adds beauty to her rooftop but also provides her with a bountiful harvest of fresh produce.

Not content with growing plants, Sarah took her commitment to sustainability a step further. She began composting her kitchen scraps, turning waste into valuable nutrients for her garden. By recycling organic matter, Sarah not only reduces the amount of waste that ends up in landfills but also enriches the soil, fostering healthy plant growth.

In her quest to minimize her environmental impact, Sarah also implemented rainwater collection systems. By harnessing the power of nature, she ensures that her garden receives ample water without relying solely on municipal resources. Sarah's innovative use of rainwater not only conserves water but also helps to reduce runoff and the strain on urban infrastructure.

But Sarah's eco-friendly practices do not stop there. Motivated by her desire to lead a sustainable lifestyle, she installed solar panels on her rooftop. These panels generate renewable energy, allowing her garden to thrive while reducing her reliance on fossil fuels. Sarah's commitment to renewable energy is not only admirable but also serves as an inspiration to others looking to make a positive impact on the environment.

Beyond the practical benefits, Sarah's rooftop garden has become a sanctuary for relaxation and a haven for pollinators. Surrounded by vibrant colors and the soothing sounds of nature, Sarah finds solace and tranquility in her rooftop oasis. Her garden serves as a vital resource for pollinators such as bees and butterflies, creating a thriving ecosystem that supports biodiversity in the city's heart.

In conclusion, Sarah's rooftop garden is a testament to the power of passion, dedication, and sustainable practices. Through her love for gardening and her commitment to environmental stewardship, she has successfully created a vibrant and eco-friendly space that not only brings her joy but also contributes to a greener and more sustainable future. Sarah's journey serves as an inspiration to all who aspire to transform their surroundings into a haven of beauty, sustainability, and biodiversity.

John and his family made a conscious decision to adopt a zero-waste lifestyle to reduce their environmental footprint and live more sustainably. They understood that single-use plastics were a major contributor to waste and pollution, so they started by minimizing their usage of such items. They replaced plastic water bottles with reusable ones, switched from plastic grocery bags to cloth bags, and began carrying their own reusable coffee cups and cutlery.

But their journey towards zero waste did not stop there. John and his family recognized many other products in their daily lives as difficult to recycle or reuse. So, they gradually committed to eliminating these items. They started by carefully examining their purchasing habits and opting for products with minimal or no packaging. They also began buying in bulk at stores that allowed them to bring their own containers, reducing the need for excessive packaging.

Besides reducing their waste through smart shopping choices, John and his family took it a step further by making their own cleaning products. John and his family discovered that many household cleaners contain harmful chemicals and often come in plastic containers. By creating their own cleaning solutions using simple ingredients, they not only eliminated the need for these harmful products but also significantly reduced their waste output.

Their efforts paid off, as over time, John and his family could reduce their household waste to just a small jar of trash each year. This remarkable achievement not only brought them a sense of accomplishment, but also inspired them to share their experiences with others. They became advocates for sustainable living, organizing workshops and presentations in their community to educate others on the benefits of reducing waste and providing practical tips on how to incorporate zero-waste practices into their daily lives.

John and his family's dedication to living a zero-waste lifestyle has had a ripple effect in their community. By leading by example and showcasing the positive impact of their choices, they have inspired many others to join the movement and adopt more sustainable practices. Their efforts have sparked a wave of change, with more and more individuals and families taking steps towards reducing waste and embracing a lifestyle that prioritizes environmental responsibility.

In Kenya, a group of passionate and committed volunteers embarked on a transformative reforestation project in a region severely affected by rampant deforestation. Recognizing the urgent need to address this environmental crisis, they began their mission by planting a diverse range of native trees, carefully selected to restore the ecological balance disturbed over the years. However, their efforts extended far beyond merely planting trees; they recognized the importance of education and community involvement in achieving long-term sustainability. Thus, they engaged with the local community, conducting workshops and awareness programs to promote a deep understanding of the significance of conservation.

As time passed, the dedication and perseverance of these volunteers bore fruit. The once degraded land regenerated, with vibrant new growth emerging from the soil. Biodiversity, once on the brink of collapse, experienced a remarkable revival, as various plant and animal species found new habitats in the rejuvenated environment. This ecological restoration not only benefited the natural world but also had a profound impact on the lives of the local people.

With the revival of the land, the local community witnessed a resurgence of economic opportunities and improved livelihoods. The reforested areas provided a source of sustainable income through activities such as eco-tourism, beekeeping, and the production of indigenous herbal remedies. These newfound economic avenues not only eased poverty but also empowered the local population, enabling them to take ownership of their natural resources and actively take part in the conservation efforts.

News of this remarkable project spread, captivating the hearts and minds of more individuals who yearned to make a difference. The project, once started by a small group of volunteers, grew exponentially. With each passing year, more volunteers joined the cause, expanding the reforestation efforts to other regions in Kenya. Regenerated forests, rebounding wildlife populations, and more resilient communities facing environmental challenges increasingly showed the impact of this collective endeavor.

Today, this reforestation project stands as a testament to the power of community-driven initiatives and the remarkable resilience of nature. It serves as an inspiring example of how a small group of dedicated individuals can create a ripple effect of positive change, not only restoring the land but also fostering a deep sense of environmental stewardship within communities.

Anna, a resident of a small village in Germany, has emerged as a catalyst for change in her community's transition to clean energy. Through her unwavering dedication and leadership, she has successfully organized initiatives that have not only educated her neighbors about renewable energy sources but also led to the installation of wind turbines and solar panels. As a result, the village now produces more energy than it consumes, setting an example for other communities striving to reduce their carbon footprint. This narrative serves to highlight the power of individual actions in effecting significant positive changes and emphasizes the importance of every effort in caring for our planet.

Anna recognized the urgent need to address the environmental challenges facing her village and took matters into her own hands. She began by organizing workshops to educate her neighbors about the benefits of renewable energy sources. These sessions covered topics such as solar power, wind energy, and the importance of reducing reliance on fossil fuels. By fostering awareness and understanding, Anna successfully instilled a sense of urgency and responsibility within her community.

Eager to put her knowledge into action, Anna collaborated with local authorities to spearhead the installation of wind turbines and solar panels throughout the village. With her persuasive skills and unwavering determination, she convinced the authorities of the long-term economic and environmental benefits of clean energy. The successful implementation of these projects not only reduced the community's carbon footprint but also generated surplus energy, enabling the village to contribute to the regional power grid.

The impact of Anna's efforts extends beyond her village, as her community has become a model for other towns and villages seeking to transition to clean energy. Many delegations from neighboring communities and even from other countries have visited Anna's village to learn from their success story. Anna and her group have encouraged others to act in their own communities by sharing their advice and what works well.

Anna's leadership and dedication have played a pivotal role in transforming her small German village into a shining example of a sustainable and environmentally conscious community. Her initiatives, from educational workshops to the installation of renewable energy infrastructure, have not only empowered her neighbors but also attracted attention and admiration from other communities worldwide. These stories reinforce the notion that individual actions, no matter how small, can lead to significant positive changes and serve as a reminder of the collective responsibility we all share in caring for our planet. Whether it is starting a small garden, reducing waste, planting trees, or advocating for clean energy, every effort counts in building a sustainable future.

Some of the impactful things my wife and I are doing to live more responsible lives is to unplug all unnecessary things in our home. For example, we have unplugged clocks in our extra bedrooms where no one sleeps. It may not make a ton of difference, but will ease our demand for more power. This lessens the demands for more fossil fuels.

Another thing we are doing is to park one of our two vehicles and carpooling together when we need to drive to town for shopping, etc. This saves more fuel during the year, as well as more fossil fuels from being burned.

At our home, we have embarked on an exciting journey of transforming a significant portion of our front lawn into a vibrant and flourishing wildflower garden. This endeavor not only brings aesthetic appeal but also contributes to a variety of environmental benefits. By reducing the grassy area, we will not only reduce the time and effort spent on lawn maintenance but also play our part in conserving natural resources, such as fuel. Introducing pollinating flowers will provide a much-needed habitat for bees, butterflies, and other critters, further enhancing the ecological balance within our surroundings. It is our firm belief that each individual can play a vital role in restoring the world to its inherent beauty and functionality, as intended by a higher power.

By converting a significant portion of our front lawn

into a wildflower garden, we aim to reduce the amount of grass that requires regular mowing and maintenance.

This reduction in grassy area not only saves us time and effort but also minimizes the consumption of fossil fuels, as fewer mowing sessions will be necessary.

The resulting decrease in fuel consumption contributes to reducing our carbon footprint, aligning with our commitment to environmental sustainability.

Our wildflower garden will serve as a haven for bees, butterflies, and other pollinators that play a crucial role in the ecosystem.

By planting a diverse range of pollinating flowers, we aim to attract these beneficial insects, ensuring their survival and promoting biodiversity.

The presence of pollinators in our garden will aid in the reproduction of plants, including neighboring gardens and local flora, ultimately contributing to the overall health and vitality of the ecosystem.

We firmly believe that everyone has the power to make a positive impact on the environment and restore the world to its intended beauty and functionality.

By transforming our front lawn into a wildflower garden, we are taking a small yet significant step towards this goal.

The beauty of wildflowers, with their vibrant colors and delicate blooms, will not only enhance the aesthetic appeal of our surroundings but also serve as a visual reminder of the inherent beauty found in nature.

Pollinator activity, by promoting plant growth, will enhance ecosystem functionality and ensure a sustainable environment for all living organisms.

In conclusion, the decision to transform a substantial portion of our front lawn into a wildflower garden represents our commitment to environmental sustainability and the restoration of nature's beauty and functionality. By reducing grassy areas, we save time, effort, and fuel consumption, while simultaneously providing a habitat for important pollinators. We believe that these small actions, when multiplied across communities, can create a significant positive impact, contributing to a more balanced and thriving natural world.

One important book recommendation in helping you deal with this chapter would be my favorite book on the subject:

Serve God, Save the Planet: A Christian Call to Action, by Matthew Sleeth, MD. It is published by Zondervan and may be ordered from Amazon or other book-sellers.

4

Social Justice and Human Rights

IN TIMOTHY KELLER'S BOOK, *Generous Justice**, he explores the concept of justice from a Christian perspective. Keller delves into the idea that justice is not simply a legal or social construct, but a reflection of God's character and desire for the world. He argues that, as believers, we are called to pursue and actively promote justice in all areas of life, including our relationships, communities, and society. Keller challenges readers to consider the biblical mandate to care for the marginalized, oppressed, and vulnerable, emphasizing the importance of generosity in our pursuit of justice. Through engaging storytelling, theological insights, and practical examples, *Generous Justice* offers an interesting and thought-provoking exploration of the role of justice in the Christian faith.

On the topic of social justice, it is crucial to address the systemic inequalities and injustices prevalent in society. Fair treatment for everyone, regardless of race, gender, socioeconomic status, or other personal characteristics, is the goal of social justice advocates. It aims to dismantle discriminatory systems and structures that perpetuate oppression and limit opportunities for marginalized communities. This includes advocating for equal access to education, healthcare, employment, and legal protection. Social justice also involves recognizing and challenging implicit biases and prejudices that perpetuate discrimination and injustice. It emphasizes the importance of promoting diversity, inclusion, and representation in all aspects of society. By striving for social justice, we can create a more equitable and just world for everyone.

Lisa, an impassioned environmental activist, became deeply concerned when she discovered the stark reality that low-income communities in her city were enduring pollution. Keenly aware of the detrimental health effects and overall quality of life implications, she embarked on a mission to shed light on this injustice.

Lisa understood that to effect change, she needed to empower and collaborate with the very residents who were experiencing the detrimental effects of environmental hazards firsthand. Together, they undertook a rigorous documentation process, meticulously cataloging the various pollutants and their sources in these communities.

Armed with their findings, Lisa fearlessly approached city officials, determined to present an undeniable case for immediate action. Through her eloquent and unwavering advocacy, she captured the attention and empathy of those in power. As a result, city officials imposed stricter regulations on polluting industries, forcing them to adopt more sustainable and environmentally friendly practices. Tangible improvements in the affected neighborhoods resulted from the allocation of resources to address existing pollution and its consequences.

Lisa's remarkable work served as an important reminder of the intrinsic connection between environmental and social justice. Lisa, through her support of clean air and water, showed that these necessities are fundamental human rights, not luxuries, and must be protected by everyone.

Ideas for Social Justice and Human Rights:

1. **Volunteer with Local Organizations:** One way to make a meaningful impact in your community

is by joining local organizations that advocate for marginalized communities. Consider getting involved with organizations such as homeless shelters, food banks, or advocacy groups that work tirelessly to address the needs and challenges faced by these communities. By dedicating your time and effort as a volunteer, you can directly contribute to providing help, support, and resources to those who need it most. Not only will this experience allow you to make a positive difference in the lives of others, but it will also provide you with a deeper understanding of the issues faced by marginalized communities.

2. **Educate Yourself and Others:** Another essential step in promoting social justice is to educate yourself about the various issues and challenges surrounding marginalized communities. By staying informed about current social justice issues, you can better comprehend the root causes of inequality and discrimination. This knowledge will enable you to engage in meaningful conversations and discussions with friends, family, and

colleagues, helping to raise awareness and promote understanding. By sharing your knowledge and insights, you can inspire others to take action and join the fight for social justice. It is through education and open dialogue that we can create a more inclusive and equitable society for all.

3. **Support Fair Trade:** Purchase products that are ethically sourced and support fair wages for workers. Fair trade is a movement that aims to promote social and economic justice by ensuring that producers, especially those in developing countries, receive fair compensation for their labor. When you choose to buy fair trade products, you are actively supporting a system that prioritizes the well-being of workers and communities.

Fair trade certification ensures environmentally sustainable and socially responsible production of the products you buy. The fair-trade certification pays fair wages to workers involved in the production process. Fair trade organizations often invest in community development projects, such as education, healthcare, and infrastructure, to improve the livelihoods of the communities they work with.

By supporting fair trade, you are making a conscious choice to contribute to a fairer global economy. You are supporting small-scale farmers and artisans who often face significant challenges in accessing markets and negotiating fair prices for their products. Fair trade empowers these producers to have a voice in the global marketplace and enables them to improve their economic prospects and quality of life.

When you purchase fair trade products, you are not only making a positive impact on individuals and communities around the world, but you are also embracing sustainability. Fair trade promotes environmentally friendly practices, such as organic farming and reducing the use of harmful chemicals, which help protect ecosystems and preserve biodiversity.

So, next time you go shopping, consider choosing fair trade products. By doing so, you are using your purchasing power to support ethical practices, fair wages, and sustainable development. Together, we can create a more just and fairer world for all.

Advocate for Policy Changes: Get involved in local and national politics to push for laws that protect human rights. Actively taking part in the political process and engaging with elected officials and policymakers is one way to make a significant impact.

Begin by researching your community's current human rights landscape and identifying specific areas needing policy changes. This could include issues such as discrimination, access to healthcare, affordable housing, or criminal justice reform. Educate yourself on relevant laws and regulations, as well as the positions of different political parties and candidates on these issues. Attend town hall meetings, community forums, and public hearings to voice your concerns and advocate for protecting human rights.

Join or form advocacy groups focused on human rights to amplify your voice and collaborate with like-minded individuals. Use various communication channels, such as writing letters, making phone calls, or sending emails, to reach out to your elected representatives and express your support for specific policy changes. Building relationships with policymakers and their staff can also be beneficial in advancing your cause. By actively taking part in the political process, you can help shape the laws and policies that safeguard human rights and create a more just and equitable society for all.

Mentor and Empower Youth: Support young people from disadvantaged backgrounds through mentorship programs. We recognize the importance of investing in the future of our youth, especially those facing significant challenges because of their disadvantaged backgrounds. Through mentorship programs, we aim to provide guidance, support, and empowerment to these young individuals, equipping them with the tools to overcome obstacles and achieve their full potential. By pairing them with caring and committed mentors, we strive to create a positive impact on their lives and contribute to a more inclusive and equitable society.

Maria, an immigrant, volunteers with a local immigrant rights organization. She helps newcomers navigate the legal system, find housing, and access to education. One day, she met a family who had fled their home country because of violence. Maria's efforts helped them secure legal status, and now the children are thriving in school, and the parents have stable jobs. This experience reinforced Maria's belief in the importance of standing up for immigrant rights.

James, a passionate and dedicated high school teacher, noticed that his school, Lincoln High, had a significant achievement gap between students of different racial backgrounds. Concerned by this disparity, James took matters into his own hands and address the issue head-on. He envisioned an after-school tutoring program that would provide extra support to students who needed it the most. With unwavering determination, James tirelessly worked to bring his vision to life. He collaborated with fellow teachers, administrators, and community members to create a comprehensive program that would bridge the gap and empower students to reach their fullest potential.

As word spread about James's innovative tutoring program, more teachers and community volunteers eagerly joined forces to make a difference in the lives of these students. They wanted to make sure all students had an equal chance of success, no matter their race. Together, they developed personalized learning plans, conducted individualized tutoring sessions, and provided a safe and nurturing environment for students to flourish academically.

The impact of James's program was nothing short of remarkable. Over time, students who were previously struggling thrived, their grades improved, and their confidence soared. The once-widening achievement gap narrowed, and students of all racial backgrounds achieved academic excellence. Beyond the tangible academic progress, the program fostered a sense of belonging and empowerment among the students, instilling in them the belief that their dreams were within reach.

James's unwavering dedication to racial equality and educational equity made a lasting and tangible difference in the Lincoln High School community. His program not only transformed the lives of individual students but also served as a catalyst for change within the school system. The success of the program inspired other schools in the district to adopt similar initiatives, further amplifying the impact and driving positive change throughout the entire community.

James's story is a testament to the power of one person's commitment to making a difference. His tireless efforts and belief inspire educators, students, and community members in each student's potential. Through his program, he proved that with the right support, resources, and unwavering determination, it is possible to bridge the achievement gap and create a more equitable and inclusive educational environment for all.

Emily, an outspoken advocate and ally of the LGBTQ+ community, recognized the need for a supportive and inclusive environment for LGBTQ+ employees at her workplace. Motivated by her own experiences and the experiences shared by her friends and colleagues, Emily acted. She started a support group within the company, dedicated to providing a safe space for LGBTQ+ individuals to share their stories, seek guidance, and build a network of support.

To ensure the success of the support group, Emily organized regular workshops and events focused on educating colleagues about LGBTQ+ issues, fostering understanding, and promoting inclusivity. These sessions covered a wide range of topics, including pronoun usage, legal protections, and the challenges faced by the LGBTQ+ community. By creating an open and non-judgmental atmosphere, Emily encouraged dialogue and encouraged colleagues to ask questions, facilitating a deeper understanding of the LGBTQ+ experience.

The impact of Emily's efforts was profound. One colleague, who had been struggling with their identity and had felt isolated and misunderstood, found the courage to come out within the supportive space created by the support group. This newfound sense of acceptance and support at work came from the individual's knowledge that accepting colleagues surrounded them. The support group became a beacon of hope and solidarity for LGBTQ+ employees, allowing them to express their authentic selves without fear of judgment or discrimination.

Through Emily's dedication and passion, the workplace underwent a significant transformation. The support group not only created a more inclusive environment, but it also helped individuals feel respected for who they are. Colleagues began actively engaging in conversations about LGBTQ+ issues, demonstrating increased awareness and empathy towards the unique challenges faced by the community. The ripple effect of Emily's initiative extended beyond the confines of the workplace, influencing the overall culture of the company and inspiring other organizations to establish similar support systems.

Emily's story exemplifies the power of ally-ship and the positive impact that one individual can have on the lives of others. Through her unwavering commitment, she not only created a safe space for LGBTQ+ employees but also fostered a culture of inclusivity and acceptance that will continue to thrive long after her departure. Her work shows that minor acts of kindness and understanding can make an enormous difference for marginalized people, and that workplaces can become places where everyone feels valued and appreciated for who they are.

Social justice and human rights are two interconnected concepts that are at the core of a fair society. Social justice refers to the concept of ensuring that every individual has equal access to opportunities, resources, and privileges, regardless of their background or identity. It aims to address and rectify social inequalities and systemic injustices that exist within society.

Being human entitles every person to human rights—fundamental rights and freedoms. These rights encompass a wide range of areas, including civil, political, economic, social, and cultural rights. Upholding and protecting the human rights of all individuals is the central focus of the pursuit of social justice.

Social justice strives to build a society that respects, protects, and fulfills the human rights of everyone, regardless of their race, gender, religion, or socioeconomic status. Together, social justice and human rights form the foundation for a just and inclusive society, where everyone can thrive and live a dignified life.

Isaiah 1:17: "Learn to do right; seek justice. Defend the oppressed. Take up the cause of the fatherless; plead the case of the widow."

Proverbs 31:8-9: "Speak up for those who cannot speak for themselves, for the rights of all who are destitute. Speak up and judge fairly; defend the rights of the poor and needy."

Matthew 25:35-40 reads: "For I was hungry, and you gave me food, I was thirsty and you gave me drink, I was a stranger and you invited me in, I needed clothes and you clothed me, I was sick and you looked after me, I was in prison and you came to see me … The King will reply, 'Truly I tell you, whatever you did for one of the least of these brothers and sisters of mine, you did for me.'"

James 1:27 in the Bible highlights the religion that God our Father accepts as pure and faultless. According to this verse, true religion involves two fundamental aspects. It calls for the care and support of orphans and widows in their distress. This emphasizes the importance of showing compassion, empathy, and practical help to those who are vulnerable and in need. It emphasizes the significance of maintaining one's personal purity and integrity amidst the corrupting influences of the world. This implies that individuals should strive to resist the negative temptations and sinful behaviors prevalent in society, and instead, live a life that is pleasing to God.

This verse serves as a guide for believers, encouraging them to prioritize acts of kindness and service towards the less fortunate, while also remaining steadfast in their faith and moral values.

These suggestions will help us better ourselves and the world.

****You may purchase *Generous Justice* by Timothy Keller, Penguin Books, 2016, from Amazon, Books a Million, and other bookstores for further reading options on this topic.

5

Technology, Ethics, and Digital Evangelism

Artificial Intelligence (AI), an advanced branch of computer science, has become increasingly prevalent in various aspects of our daily lives. From smartphones to smart homes, AI technology has seamlessly integrated into our environment, transforming the way we interact with machines and enhancing our overall experiences.

AI is now an essential component of many industries, including healthcare, finance, transportation, and entertainment. It has revolutionized medical diagnostics, enabling doctors to make accurate diagnoses and develop personalized treatment plans. In the financial sector, AI algorithms analyze vast amounts of data to detect patterns and make informed investment decisions.

AI-powered autonomous vehicles are paving the way for safer and more efficient transportation systems. AI has made significant contributions to the entertainment industry, from personalized movie recommendations to virtual reality gaming experiences. With its ability to process and understand complex information, AI has become an indispensable tool for businesses and individuals alike.

The ethical implications of AI are important to consider. What are they? As artificial intelligence continues to advance and become more integrated into our daily lives, it raises important ethical questions that need to be addressed. One concern is the potential for AI to replace human workers, leading to job displacement and economic inequality.

Another ethical consideration is bias in AI algorithms, which can perpetuate discrimination and reinforce existing societal inequalities. Using AI in surveillance and privacy invasion raises concerns about individual rights and freedoms.

The development of autonomous AI systems raises questions about accountability and responsibility for their actions. These ethical implications cause careful regulation and oversight to ensure AI technology aligns with ethical principles and respects human values. Who is watching out for this? Who makes certain that AI helps and does not damage us?

In the realm of artificial intelligence (AI), the responsibility of ensuring its beneficial and safe deployment lies in the hands of various stakeholders. One of the key entities responsible for overseeing AI's impact on society is the government. Governments play a crucial role in setting regulations and policies that govern the development, deployment, and use of AI systems. They establish ethical guidelines, privacy safeguards, and legal frameworks to protect individuals and prevent AI from being detrimental.

Academic institutions and research organizations contribute to the responsible development of AI. These institutions conduct thorough research, provide education on AI ethics, and promote interdisciplinary collaboration to address the potential risks associated with AI. They also work towards creating transparency and accountability within the AI community.

The safe and beneficial use of AI depends heavily on industry leaders and technology companies. They have a crucial role to play. Companies that develop AI technologies are increasingly adopting ethical frameworks and principles to guide their research and development efforts. They invest in robust testing and verification processes to minimize biases, mitigate risks, and enhance the overall safety of AI systems.

Non-profit organizations and advocacy groups actively monitor AI advancements and advocate for policies that prioritize human well-being. These organizations engage in public awareness campaigns, collaborate with policy-makers, and work towards creating a collective under-standing of the potential risks and benefits of AI.

Individuals themselves have a responsibility to stay in-formed about AI developments and engage in discussions about its impact on society. By participating in public forums, voicing concerns, and demanding transparency, individuals can contribute to the responsible development and deployment of AI.

AI's benefits must outweigh its potential harms. This requires collaboration between governments, academics, industries, non-profits, and individuals.

Are there factions that will use AI for detriment and how?

In the rapidly developing landscape of artificial intelligence (AI), there is a growing concern about the potential misuse of this powerful technology. While AI has the potential to revolutionize various industries and improve our lives, there are factions that may exploit it for detrimental purposes. These factions can include malicious hackers, cybercriminal organizations, or even certain governments with ulterior motives.

One way in which these factions can use AI for detriment is through the development and deployment of AI-powered cyberattacks. With AI algorithms, these malicious actors can create sophisticated and autonomous malware that can evade traditional security measures and cause widespread damage. Such attacks can target critical infrastructure, financial systems, or even personal devices, leading to disruption, financial loss, and compromising sensitive information.

Another concern is the use of AI for the creation and dissemination of misinformation and fake news. By leveraging AI algorithms, factions can generate highly convincing deep fake videos, images, or articles that can mislead and manipulate public opinion. This can have serious implications for democracy, social cohesion, and trust in institutions.

Factions may exploit AI for surveillance and invasion of privacy. By combining AI with various data sources, governments or surveillance agencies can develop advanced surveillance systems capable of monitoring individual's activities, analyzing behavior patterns, and even predicting future actions. This raises significant ethical and privacy concerns, as it infringes upon personal freedoms and civil liberties.

It is essential to recognize the potential dangers associated with the misuse of AI and work towards establishing robust regulations and ethical guidelines to prevent these factions from exploiting the technology. Governments, researchers, and industry must collaborate to ensure responsible AI development and deployment. This will help prevent its misuse.

My wife Renee and I watched a TV show a few nights ago. We were very concerned to see two passengers lose control of their car. The show we were watching was a thrilling crime drama, and this scene added an unexpected twist to the storyline.

Suddenly, someone or something began driving the car remotely. It was a jaw-dropping moment as we tried to comprehend how the vehicle could be operating on its own. The level of suspense escalated as the car maneuvered through the busy streets, narrowly avoiding collisions with other vehicles. It seemed like an invisible force had taken complete control of the car, leaving the passengers helpless and bewildered.

Tension peaked when a group of carjackers remotely drove the car into a warehouse. The unexpected turn of events left us on the edge of our seats, eagerly waiting to see how the characters would escape this perilous situation. The show's gripping plot and intricate storytelling had us captivated throughout the entire episode, and this scene left a lasting impression on both Renee and me. What does this kind of activity hold for the future? Are we losing control of everything?

How do drones fit into the arena of AI technology?

Drones have revolutionized various industries by seamlessly integrating with AI technology. These unmanned aerial vehicles have become highly intelligent and autonomous because of the advancements in artificial intelligence algorithms. With AI, drones can process vast amounts of data in real time, making them capable of performing complex tasks such as autonomous navigation, object detection, and even decision-making. AI enables drones to perceive their surroundings accurately, avoiding obstacles, and adapting to changing environments.

Drones using this technology can process data to give helpful results. This makes them useful for many things like farming, construction, security, and search and rescue. We can deploy AI-powered drones for precision delivery, monitoring, and mapping, thus enhancing efficiency and productivity in various industries. Overall, drones have seamlessly integrated with AI technology, empowering them to be more intelligent, versatile, and transformative in their applications.

But what are the detrimental factors involved in using drones?

While drones offer many benefits, such as efficiency, cost-effectiveness, and improved safety, they also come with certain drawbacks that need to be considered. One major concern is the potential invasion of privacy. Drones equipped with cameras can easily capture images or videos of individuals without their consent, raising ethical and legal questions.

There is the risk of accidents and collisions. Drones flying in crowded areas or near other aircraft can pose a significant threat to public safety. The reliance on drone technology can lead to job displacement in certain industries.

Advanced drones may replace human workers in delivery and aerial photography. This is a growing concern.

Finally, there are security risks associated with drones. These unmanned aerial vehicles can serve nefarious purposes, such as smuggling contraband, conducting surveillance for criminal activities, or even conducting terrorist attacks. Therefore, while drones offer various advantages, careful consideration of these detrimental factors is crucial, and establishing proper regulations and safeguards to mitigate any potential harm is necessary.

What are the moral dilemmas of using AI?

Artificial Intelligence (AI) has become an integrated part of our lives, revolutionizing various sectors, such as healthcare, transportation, and entertainment. However, the widespread adoption of AI has also raised several moral dilemmas that need careful consideration. One significant concern is privacy and data security. With the vast amount of data collected and analyzed by AI systems, there is a risk of unauthorized access, misuse, and potential breaches of personal information. This raises questions about the ethical responsibility of companies and organizations to protect individuals' privacy.

Another moral dilemma associated with AI is the potential for bias and discrimination. Historical data, often reflecting societal biases and prejudices, trains AI algorithms. As a result, AI systems may inadvertently perpetuate existing inequalities and discrimination, particularly in areas like hiring, lending, and law enforcement. This raises ethical concerns about fairness, justice, and equal opportunities.

The deployment of AI in autonomous systems, such as self-driving cars or military drones, raises ethical questions regarding accountability and decision-making. When accidents or harm result from AI errors or malfunctions, who is responsible? How can we ensure that AI systems make ethical decisions in critical situations? These dilemmas underscore the necessity of clear guidelines and regulations governing AI use and mitigating potential risks.

The impact of AI or employment and job displacement presents an unavoidable moral dilemma. As AI technology advances, there is a concern that it will replace human workers in various industries, leading to unemployment and economic inequality. Addressing this issue requires careful consideration of how to ensure a just transition and provide opportunities for reskilling and upskilling.

In conclusion, the moral dilemmas associated with using AI are multifaceted and require thoughtful analysis and ethical decision-making. Responsible and ethical AI requires addressing several complex issues. Among these are data security, bias, decision-making processes, and job displacement.

Technology in Church

Today's technologies have revolutionized the way churches operate and communicate with their congregations. One of the key ways technology has affected the church is through the use of social media platforms. Churches can now reach a wider audience and engage with their members through platforms such as Facebook, Instagram, and Twitter. They can share sermons, inspirational messages, and upcoming events, allowing members to stay connected even outside of traditional service times.

Technology has made it easier for churches to manage their administrative tasks. Online giving platforms enable members to donate and tithe electronically, simplifying the financial aspects of running a church. Technology has made it possible for churches to live-stream their services, reaching those who cannot physically attend because of distance or health reasons. This not only allows members to stay connected, but also opens up the opportunity for new people to discover and join the church community. Overall, the benefits of today's technologies in the church include increased outreach, improved communication, streamlined administrative processes, and enhanced accessibility for all members.

What are some drawbacks of using Church technologies?

While Church technologies have undoubtedly brought about various benefits and advancements, it is important to consider the potential drawbacks they may entail. First, one detriment is the risk of overreliance on technology, which can lead to a diminished sense of human connection and community within the church.

Digital platforms and online interactions increasingly absorb people, potentially jeopardizing the face-to-face interactions that have traditionally been central to church life.

There is accessibility and exclusion. Technology can broaden church reach, but it may also exclude those lacking access or comfort with technology. This can create a divide within the church community and hinder the inclusivity and diversity that churches strive to foster.

Finally, there are concerns related to privacy and security. With the increasing use of online platforms and data storage, there is a heightened risk of sensitive information being compromised or misused. This can undermine trust within the church community and raise ethical concerns regarding the handling of personal data. Church technologies offer many benefits, but it's important to consider potential drawbacks like less human interaction, accessibility problems, and privacy issues.

Following a recent back surgery, I was homebound for a few weeks but never missed a church service. Despite my physical limitations, I found solace because technology allowed me to stay connected with my faith community.

One of my dear friends, the Rev. Jimmy Cason, was filling a pulpit out in Mississippi, and thanks to YouTube, I could watch his church services and hear his sermons from the comfort of my home. It was incredible to witness his powerful messages, and I felt a sense of unity with the congregation, even though I could not be there in person.

My local church also used the same digital platform to livestream their services. This meant that I could take part in worship and listen to inspiring sermons right from my living room recliner! Online church services were incredibly convenient and accessible during my recovery. They helped me maintain my faith and find comfort.

This is only one of numerous highlights of today's technology the church uses to reach a larger congregation. **Digital Evangelism** has become an essential tool in spreading the message of the church to a wider audience.

With various digital platforms and social media, churches can now connect with individuals from all over the world, breaking geographical barriers and transcending traditional limitations. Online platforms like websites, podcasts, live streams, and social media allow churches to share sermons and teachings with a wider audience. This includes people who cannot attend services physically. This opens up new avenues for outreach and allows the church to engage with individuals who may seek spiritual guidance or have questions about their faith.

Digital evangelism's power is its ability to reach diverse people everywhere, offering them a platform to explore their faith. It is an exciting development that has revolutionized the way the church connects with its congregation and spreads the word of God.

A young church member mentioned how using social media platforms like Instagram and TikTok helped him share his faith with his peers. He could inspire youth by sharing his faith journey through short videos and answering questions online. This could reach those who have never been to church.

A shy church member found her voice through digital evangelism. She started a blog where she shared her individual experiences and reflections on her faith. This not only helped her grow spiritually but also encouraged others who resonated with her story to reach out and share their own experiences.

During the COVID-19 pandemic, Sarah, a dedicated and compassionate church member, recognized the growing need for emotional and spiritual support among her fellow congregants.

In response, she took it upon herself to use digital tools and technology to create virtual support groups. Sarah understood how isolation and anxiety harm mental health. Therefore, she created a safe, faith-based space for people to share their feelings.

Through her tireless efforts, she successfully organized and facilitated these virtual support groups, offering a lifeline to many who were struggling during this unprece-dented time. Sarah's unwavering commitment and empa-thetic nature allowed her to connect with individuals from all levels of society, helping them navigate the challenges of the pandemic with hope and strength. Her selflessness and dedication not only provided comfort to those in need, but also served as an inspiring example of the power of community and faith in times of crisis.

Digital evangelism has proven to be a powerful tool for spreading the message of faith and providing spiritual support, especially in times of global travel restrictions. One church member, who has been actively involved in international missions, recently shared his experience and how he could continue his important work despite the challenging circumstances. By leveraging various digital platforms, he *could* reach individuals in different countries and offer them much needed spiritual guidance.

One of the key methods he used was online sermons. Through live streaming or pre-recorded messages, he de-livered powerful and uplifting sermons to a global audi-ence. This approach allowed him to connect with peo-ple who would have otherwise been inaccessible because of geographical limitations. The ability to reach believers and non-believers alike on a virtual platform opened new avenues for sharing the gospel and offering encouragement in uncertain times.

Besides online sermons, the church member also organized virtual prayer meetings. These gatherings allowed people from various parts of the world to come together and seek solace in prayer. Despite physical distance, participants could join in a collective spiritual experience, sharing their burdens and finding strength in their faith. Using video conferencing technology enabled a sense of community and unity among believers, fostering a supportive environment even in the absence of physical proximity.

The church member harnessed the power of digital resources to provide ongoing spiritual support. By creating and sharing e-books, devotionals, and other written materials, he ensured that individuals seeking guidance had access to valuable resources at their fingertips. These digital resources were helpful for those who could not attend traditional church services or participate in physical discipleship programs. The convenience and accessibility of these materials allowed individuals to grow in their faith and deepen their understanding of spiritual principles.

In conclusion, the church member's experience highlights the transformative potential of digital evangelism. By embracing online sermons, virtual prayer meetings, and digital resources, he could continue his mission of spreading the message of faith and providing spiritual guidance to individuals across different countries. This approach not only overcame the barriers posed by travel restrictions but also opened up new opportunities to connect with believers and nonbelievers worldwide. In a world increasingly reliant on technology, digital evangelism has proven to be an invaluable tool in reaching and inspiring people through the timeless message of hope and salvation.

Balancing Tradition and Innovation

Balancing the challenges and opportunities for integrating technology with traditional faith practices can be a complex and multifaceted endeavor. As societies become increasingly digitized, religious communities face incorporating technology into their traditional practices while maintaining the essence and authenticity of their faith.

Integrating technology can bring about numerous benefits, such as improved communication, accessibility, and outreach. For instance, live streaming religious services allow individuals who cannot physically attend to still participate in worship.

Online platforms and social media enable religious organizations to connect with a wider audience and engage in meaningful dialogue. However, this integration also presents challenges requiring careful navigation. One of the major concerns is the potential dilution of religious experiences and rituals because of the intrusion of technology.

Finding a balance between leveraging technology to enhance religious practices and protecting their sanctity and spiritual essence is crucial. Addressing issues of privacy, security, and potential technology misuse within religious contexts is crucial. Integrating technology with traditional faith is challenging, but offers opportunities. Thoughtful consideration, open dialogue, and adaptability is key to success.

Scriptural References:

I. **Great Commission:** *"Go therefore and make disciples of all nations, baptizing them in the name of the Father and of the Son and of the Holy Spirit, teaching them to observe all that I have commanded you."* (Matthew 28: 19-20)

o **Idea:** Use AI to translate and disseminate evangelistic materials in multiple languages, reaching people across the globe.

2. **Parable of the Sower:** *"A sower went out to sow his seed. As he sowed, some fell along the path and was trampled underfoot, and the birds of the air devoured it.* "(Luke 8:5)

o **Idea:** Create engaging and interactive Bible study apps that help individuals understand and retain the teachings of the Bible.

3. **Paul's Use of Technology:** "I *have become all things to all people, that by all means I might save some."* (I Corinthians 9:22)

Paul, an apostle of Jesus Christ, was a fervent advocate for using technology to spread the message of salvation to as many people as possible. In his letter to the Corinthians, Paul expressed his willingness to adapt to and embrace various technological tools for effectively connecting with diverse audiences. By stating, "I have become all things to all people, that by all means I might save some," Paul showed his commitment to using technology as a powerful tool for evangelism. He recognized each person has unique preferences and ways of accessing information, and he was determined to meet people where they were by leveraging technology.

Paul's understanding of the importance of technology in spreading the Gospel underscores his dedication to reaching people from diverse backgrounds and cultures, leading them to salvation. Whether it was through the written word, letters, or even face-to-face conversations facilitated by technology, Paul made use of every available means to share the message of Christ's love and redemption.

*** An outstanding book to read on this subject is *God, Technology, and the Christian Life* by Tony Reinke. Crossway, Wheaton, IL. You may purchase a copy at all your favorite booksellers.

6

Cultural Connections and Pop Culture

W E WILL DISCUSS THE following topics in this chapter.

*Christian Themes in Media

*Interfaith Dialogues

*Influence on Society

*Art and Faith

Section 1: Christian Themes in Media

First, let us delve into the fascinating world of Christian themes across various forms of media. These portrayals can vary widely, reflecting both positive and negative aspects.

MOVIES

Positive Representations:

Mel Gibson's 2004 film, ***The Passion of the Christ,*** is

a critically acclaimed depiction of Jesus' final 12 hours. It covers his arrest through his crucifixion. The film intensely portrays Jesus' physical and emotional suffering, especially during his crucifixion. It vividly captures his pain and anguish.

The Passion of Christ uses stunning visuals and powerful acting to explore themes of sacrifice, redemption, and love central to Jesus' teachings. The film fully immerses the audience in these profound themes.

It explores the ultimate sacrifice Jesus made for humanity, as well as the profound love and forgiveness he displayed towards his persecutors. By highlighting the spiritual significance of these events, the film invites viewers to reflect on their own faith and the enduring impact of Jesus' life and teachings.

The Passion of Christ is a visually stunning and thought-provoking cinematic masterpiece that leaves a lasting impression on all who experience it.

"The Chronicles of Narnia" is a film series that was released between 2005 and 2010. These films are adaptations of the beloved books written by C.S. Lewis. The series beautifully incorporates allegories of Christ and Christian values throughout the storyline. One captivat-

ing aspect of the movies is the portrayal of Asian, a prominent character who symbolizes Jesus in the Narnia universe. This representation adds depth and meaning to the narrative, as viewers can witness the embodiment of Jesus' teachings and sacrifice through this fascinating character. The Chronicles of Narnia films have captivated audiences with their powerful storytelling and profound exploration of Christian themes.

Negative Representations:

Martin Scorsese's 1988 film, **The Last Temptation of Christ**, depicts Jesus' humanity. Its unconventional portrayal sparked controversy and accusations of blasphemy.

The Da Vinci Code (2006): While popular, the film based on Dan Brown's novel faced backlash for its speculative and critical perspective on Christian history and doctrine.

I have a fascinating love for the movies and usually find something meaningful and instructive in each. Movies have the power to captivate and inspire, offering a unique form of storytelling that can resonate with people from all walks of life.

Movies offer something for everyone. Pastors can find sermon illustrations, while others may gain insights into the human experience or enjoy the entertainment. They can provide valuable life lessons, explore complex themes and emotions, and spark conversations about important social issues.

From thought-provoking dramas to light-hearted comedies, the diverse range of films available allows individuals to explore different perspectives and expand their understanding of the world. Whether it is the powerful performances, breathtaking visuals, or compelling narratives, there is something in movies for everyone to connect with and take away a meaningful experience.

MUSIC

My love for music has been a lifelong passion that has shaped my life in countless ways. I started playing music in the 1960s, joining a rock band. After turning eighteen and becoming a Christian, I pursued gospel music and solo work. I have written hundreds of songs for various artists, including myself, and recorded seventeen albums of original music. My compositional work includes an Easter Cantata crafted specifically for choir performance, besides a collection of church anthems designed for use on Sunday mornings. My professional work has gained significant recognition through widespread publication in many academic and professional journals.

Positive Representations:

Amazing Grace has inspired countless artists across genres to create their own versions. Its powerful lyrics and haunting melody have made it a timeless favorite in the world of music.

As a minister, I have had the privilege of performing this beloved hymn at numerous funerals throughout my ministry. The soothing and comforting words of "Amazing Grace" have provided solace to grieving hearts and served as a reminder of God's unending love and mercy. This hymn's message of hope and grace transcends its setting and touches listeners, whether sung traditionally or in contemporary arrangements.

Kanye West's "Jesus Walks" uniquely combines hip-hop rhythms and a powerful message about faith and personal struggles. It emphasizes the importance of divine guidance. "Jesus Walks," a contemporary Kanye West track, combines hip-hop with a powerful message of faith, struggle, and the importance of divine guidance.

Negative Representations:

The Rolling Stones' ***"Sympathy for the Devil,"*** while iconic, is controversial because of its portrayal of the devil and its questioning of religious narratives.

Black Metal Genre: Its dark and intense sound characterizes the black metal genre, often featuring fast and aggressive guitar riffs, blast beats, and harsh vocals. It emerged in the 1980s in Norway, with bands like Mayhem and Gorgoroth being at the forefront.

One distinctive aspect of black metal is its tendency to incorporate anti-Christian sentiments and imagery, which should challenge and provoke established religious beliefs. The genre's offensive nature reflects the bands' rebellion against societal norms. It also creates a dark and chaotic atmosphere. However, it is important to note that not all black metal bands adhere to these themes, as the genre has evolved and diversified to include various subgenres and musical influences.

We, as parents, should know what our children and teens are listening to on the radio, Tic-Toc, or YouTube. Some songs they may hear can be detrimental.

LITERATURE

I love books! Loan me one and I will quickly devour it. I have been reading all my life and have closely followed Christian readings and books that support the Christian faith.

Positive Representations:

"The Chronicles of Narnia" is a beloved series of fantasy novels written by C.S. Lewis. Set in the magical land of Narnia, these books have captivated readers of all ages with their enchanting storytelling and imaginative world-building. However, what sets these books apart is their underlying Christian allegory.

Lewis masterfully interweaves profound themes of sacrifice, resurrection, and the eternal battle between good and evil throughout the series. Each book in the series explores these themes uniquely, drawing parallels to biblical stories and teachings. In Narnia, readers join the Pevensie children and other characters. The story explores themes of faith, redemption, and the victory of good over evil. The Chronicles of Narnia not only entertain but also inspire readers to reflect on deeper spiritual truths, making them timeless classics in the realm of fantasy literature.

"Pilgrim's Progress" by John Bunyan is a renowned literary masterpiece that has stood the test of time. Originally published in 1678, this classic work is an allegory of the Christian journey, following the protagonist, Christian, as he embarks on a perilous pilgrimage towards the Celestial City. As Christian navigates through various ob-

stacles and encounters a diverse cast of characters, Bunyan skillfully weaves together a tapestry of spiritual lessons and moral guidance.

The novel explores themes of faith, salvation, temptation, and perseverance, making it a profound and thought-provoking read for readers of all ages. "Pilgrim's Progress's" enduring popularity stems from its universal appeal and timeless messages, continuing to resonate with readers today.

Negative Representations:

"The Da Vinci Code" by Dan Brown is a bestselling thriller novel that was later adapted into a film. This captivating story delves into the realms of mystery, religion, and art, questioning long-established Christian doctrines and presenting an alternative history that has sparked controversy and debate among readers.

Through its intricate plot and thought-provoking narrative, the novel challenges traditional beliefs and offers a fresh perspective on the life of Jesus Christ and the role of the Catholic Church. While some readers appreciate the novel's ability to stimulate critical thinking and encourage exploration of different interpretations, others find its themes and alternative theories disrespectful to their religious beliefs.

Regardless of one's personal views, "The Da Vinci Code" undeniably captivates readers with its blend of historical fiction, suspenseful storytelling, and thought-provoking ideas.

"The Satanic Verses" is a novel written by Salman Rushdie, a British Indian author. Published in 1988, the book quickly gained international attention, sparking controversy and debate. The story revolves around two characters, Gibreel Firishta and Saladin Chamcha, who survive a plane explosion over the English Channel. As they miraculously survive the crash, they experience strange and supernatural occurrences.

In his work, Rushdie masterfully combines magical realism, mythology, and historical events to explore themes of identity, religion, and cultural conflict. The novel's title, "Satanic Verses," alludes to a controversial Islamic historical incident. The Prophet Muhammad supposedly added verses to the Quran, later deemed satanic. This book is not only a work of fiction but also serves as a critique of religious fundamentalism and a reflection on the complexities of cultural integration and assimilation.

Overall, the portrayal of Christian themes in media can

be both a source of inspiration and controversy. The diversity in representation reflects the complexity and multi-faceted nature of Christianity as it intersects with culture, art, and belief.

Various forms of media, including movies, television shows, literature, music, and visual art, depict Christian themes. These portrayals often explore different aspects of the faith, such as the life of Jesus Christ, biblical stories, religious rituals, and moral teachings.

Some media productions aim to inspire and uplift audiences, emphasizing the values of love, forgiveness, and redemption that are central to the Christian faith. They may present stories of personal transformation, divine intervention, or the triumph of good over evil. Such portrayals can provide comfort, hope, and guidance to viewers, particularly those who identify as Christians. The portrayal of Christian themes in media can also generate controversy and debate. Some productions may challenge traditional interpretations of religious texts or explore more complex and nuanced aspects of the faith, which can spark discussions among believers.

Media representations of Christianity sometimes perpetuate stereotypes or misrepresentations, leading to criticism and backlash from religious communities. The portrayal of Christian themes in media is an ongoing dialogue between creators, audiences, and religious institutions, reflecting the ever-evolving relationship between faith and popular culture.

Section 2: Interfaith Dialogues

Interfaith dialogues play a crucial role in fostering peace, understanding, and cooperation among diverse faith communities. These dialogues provide a platform for individuals from different religious backgrounds to come together and engage in open and respectful discussions.

By promoting dialogue, interfaith dialogues help break down barriers and misconceptions that may exist between different faith communities. They allow participants to gain a deeper understanding of each other's beliefs, practices, and values, fostering empathy and tolerance.

Interfaith dialogues encourage collaboration and cooperation between religious groups, leading to joint efforts in addressing common social issues, such as poverty, inequality, and environmental sustainability. Through these dialogues, individuals can also learn from the spiritual wisdom and teachings of various faith traditions, enriching their own spiritual journeys.

Ultimately, interfaith dialogues contribute to building a more inclusive and harmonious society, where people of different religions can coexist peacefully and work together for the betterment of all.

A. Promoting Peace

We can promote peace through **conflict resolution**. One effective approach is through interfaith dialogues, which play a vital role in mitigating religious conflicts. These dialogues provide a platform for individuals from diverse faith communities to come together and engage in open and honest communication. By sharing their beliefs, experiences, and perspectives, participants can develop a deeper understanding and appreciation of each other's religious traditions. This fosters mutual respect and empathy, reducing the likelihood of misunderstandings that might escalate into conflicts. Interfaith dialogues also provide an opportunity for participants to address and resolve existing tensions or disputes in a peaceful and constructive manner. Through this process, individuals can find common ground and work towards building peaceful coexistence and harmony among different religious communities.

B. Building Trust

Consistent dialogues build trust among communities, creating a foundation for peaceful coexistence. Trust is essential for any collaborative effort to address social and political issues. When individuals engage in open and honest conversations, they establish a sense of mutual understanding and respect. This allows for the exploration of diverse perspectives and the sharing of personal experiences.

Through dialogue, communities can find common ground and work towards shared goals. Trust also fosters a sense of belonging and safety, as individuals feel comfortable expressing their thoughts and concerns without fear of judgment or reprisal. By building trust through ongoing dialogue, communities can navigate differences and find meaningful solutions to complex problems. This process strengthens social cohesion and promotes inclusivity and equality because the community hears and values all voices.

Trust-building dialogues enable the identification of shared values and aspirations, which can foster a sense of collective identity and purpose. Consistent dialogue builds resilient, harmonious communities. These communities can then address challenges and work toward a more just and peaceful society.

C. Fostering Understanding

Breaking Stereotypes: These dialogues offer opportunities to dispel myths and stereotypes about different religions. By learning about each other's beliefs and practices, individuals can appreciate the diversity and commonalities among different faiths. This book aims to promote interfaith understanding and acceptance by providing a platform for open and respectful discussions about various religious traditions.

Through these dialogues, we hope to challenge preconceived notions and foster a sense of unity among people of different religious backgrounds. By sharing personal experiences, knowledge, and insights, participants can acquire a deeper understanding of each other's faiths and build bridges of empathy and tolerance. In doing so, we strive to create a more inclusive and harmonious society that celebrates the rich tapestry of religious diversity.

Education and Awareness: Interfaith interactions enhance religious literacy, helping people understand the historical, cultural, and theological contexts of various religions. This knowledge is key to fostering empathy and solidarity among individuals from different religious backgrounds.

By engaging in interfaith dialogue and learning, individuals can acquire a deeper understanding of the beliefs, practices, and rituals of diverse religions. This increased awareness not only promotes tolerance and respect but also helps to dispel stereotypes and misconceptions that may exist.

Interfaith education fosters critical thinking and the critical evaluation of beliefs and assumptions. Through open and respectful conversations, individuals can challenge and broaden their perspectives, leading to a more inclusive and harmonious society.

Interfaith education combats religious discrimination by fostering understanding of shared values and common humanity across different faiths. Overall, education and awareness through interfaith interactions are crucial in building bridges, promoting harmony, and fostering a more inclusive and accepting world.

When I was in college, I participated in an interfaith dialogue group called "Bridging Beliefs." The group aimed to foster understanding and mutual respect among individuals from different religious backgrounds. We would meet every week in a cozy room on campus, where we would engage in thoughtful discussions about our various beliefs and practices.

One member of our group, James, stood out for his conservative upbringing and lack of exposure to people from different faith backgrounds. Coming from a close-knit community that held strong religious beliefs, James had rarely interacted with individuals who held different perspectives. Naturally, he approached our group with hesitancy and a bundle of assumptions about other religions.

However, as the weeks went by, I noticed a significant change in James. The discussions we had in our interfaith dialogue group had a profound impact on his mindset. Through these conversations, he began critically evaluating his own beliefs and assumptions. It was during a session focused on the concept of forgiveness that James had a breakthrough moment. Listening to the diverse perspectives shared by members of different faiths made him realize the limitations of his understanding. He found it eye-opening to see how various religions interpret and practice forgiveness differently.

As time went on, James became more open-minded and empathetic. The exposure to different belief systems and the friendships he developed within the group enriched his relationships with others. He learned to appreciate the beauty in diversity and to approach conversations with curiosity rather than judgment.

Taking part in this interfaith dialogue group was a transformative experience for all of us, but witnessing James' personal growth and increased understanding was particularly inspiring. It served as a reminder of the power of dialogue and the potential for positive change when individuals from diverse backgrounds come together to listen and learn from one another.

D. Encouraging Cooperation

Collaborative Efforts: Faith communities from various religious backgrounds can come together and pool their resources, knowledge, and expertise to work on shared goals such as social justice, environmental conservation, and humanitarian aid. Interfaith cooperation fosters a sense of unity and understanding among diverse religious groups, enabling them to address global challenges with more robust and innovative initiatives.

By combining their efforts, faith communities can make a significant impact in promoting equality, protecting the environment, and easing the suffering of those in need.

This collaboration also allows for a broader perspective and a more comprehensive approach to tackling complex issues, as different faith traditions bring unique perspectives and insights to the table. Through joint projects and initiatives, faith communities can amplify their impact and create positive change on a global scale.

Policy Influence: Unified interfaith voices can have a significant impact on shaping policy and advocating for inclusive and equitable laws that uphold the rights and freedoms of all religious groups. By coming together and speaking with a collective voice, representatives from various faith communities can effectively communicate their concerns, needs, and aspirations to policymakers at local, national, and international levels.

This collaborative approach allows for a broader and more comprehensive understanding of the diverse religious landscape and encourages lawmakers to consider the perspectives of different religious communities when drafting legislation.

Interfaith advocacy bridges divide and fosters mutual understanding between religious groups. This leads to policies protecting religious freedom, tolerance, and respect. Interfaith groups can pool their resources and expertise to influence policymakers. They can then present evidence and propose solutions to issues like religious discrimination and hate crimes.

Unified interfaith voices can shape a more inclusive society. They do this by actively participating in policy debates and offering informed recommendations.

E. Strenthening Community Bonds

Social Cohesion: Social cohesion refers to the sense of belonging and unity within a community, where individuals from different backgrounds and beliefs come together to form strong bonds. In order to this cohesion, regular interfaith activities and projects play a crucial role. These activities provide opportunities for people of different religions to interact, collaborate, and engage in shared experiences.

By participating in joint ventures, individuals not only learn about different faiths but also develop a deeper understanding and appreciation for one another's beliefs and traditions. These interactions break down barriers and stereotypes. This shared sense of belonging contributes to a more harmonious and inclusive society, where individuals from diverse religious backgrounds come together to work towards common goals and address societal challenges.

Emotional Support: In times of crisis, having established interfaith connections ensures communities can support each other emotionally and spiritually, enhancing resilience. These connections provide a platform for individuals of different faiths to come together and offer a shoulder to lean on, fostering a sense of unity and empathy. Through shared experiences and open dialogue, people can find solace in knowing that they are not alone in their struggles.

Interfaith connections facilitate the exchange of spiritual practices and rituals, allowing individuals to draw strength from diverse belief systems. Whether it is through prayers, meditation, or lending a listening ear, these connections create a supportive environment where individuals can find comfort and healing during challenging times. By nurturing emotional and spiritual well-being, interfaith connections play a vital role in enhancing the resilience of communities, enabling them to navigate crises with greater strength and solidarity.

F. Examples of Interfaith Initiatives

1. The Parliament of the World's Religions: an organization that brings together religious leaders and

communities from around the world to engage in dialogue and collaborative action.

2. Interfaith Youth Core (IFYC): a non-profit that works with young people to promote interfaith cooperation on college campuses and beyond.

3. United Religions Initiative (URI): a global grass-root interfaith network that aims to promote enduring, daily interfaith cooperation and reduce religiously motivated violence.

Interfaith dialogues are essential platforms that bring together individuals from different religious backgrounds to engage in meaningful conversations and discussions. These dialogues serve as a reminder that, regardless of our diverse beliefs, we are all connected by our shared humanity. Through open and respectful dialogue, participants gain a deeper understanding of each other's perspectives, fostering peace and harmony among different religious communities.

One of the primary goals of interfaith dialogues is to promote understanding and acceptance of diverse religious beliefs and practices. By creating a space for individuals to share their experiences and beliefs, these dialogues collapse barriers and promote tolerance and empathy. Participants can learn about different faith traditions, their core values, rituals, and teachings. This knowledge helps to dispel misconceptions and stereotypes, fostering an environment of mutual respect and appreciation.

Interfaith dialogues encourage cooperation and collaboration among religious communities. Participants recognize they share a collective responsibility for the well-being of their communities and the world at large. Through collaborative efforts, individuals from different faith backgrounds can work together to address common challenges such as poverty, environmental issues, and social injustice. By fostering cooperation, interfaith dialogues contribute to the creation of a more inclusive and equitable society.

Interfaith dialogues play a crucial role in promoting peace, understanding, and cooperation among individuals from diverse religious backgrounds. These dialogues remind us of our shared humanity and the collective responsibility we have towards creating a better world. By embracing diversity and engaging in respectful conversations, we can build a more harmonious and inclusive global society.

Section 3: Influence on Society

Christian values and beliefs have had a profound impact on cultural norms and societal behaviors across various civilizations and historical periods. The following points offer some insightful reflections on how these influences are demonstrably apparent in various aspects.

A. Moral and Ethical Framework

1. **Compassion and Charity**: Christianity places a strong emphasis on caring for the less fortunate, inspired by teachings like the Parable of the Good Samaritan and the concept of agape love. This has influenced the establishment of numerous charitable organizations, hospitals, and initiatives aimed at social welfare.

2. **Honesty and Integrity**: Christian teachings advocate for honesty, integrity, and ethical behavior. The Ten Commandments, for instance, stress the importance of truthfulness and respect for others' property and relationships.

B. Social Norms and Customs

1. **Holidays and Festivals**: Many Christian holidays, such as Christmas and Easter, have become

significant cultural events celebrated by people of various faiths and backgrounds. These holidays often shape societal rhythms, influencing business closures, school calendars, and public festivities.

2. **Marriage and Family**: Christian views on marriage, particularly the sanctity of the union and the traditional family structure, have historically influenced societal norms regarding family life and gender roles. Christian doctrine underpins concepts such as monogamy and lifelong marriage commitment.

C. Legal and Political Systems

Human Rights and Dignity: The concept of human rights, deeply rooted in the belief in the sanctity of human life, has been a driving force behind various international and national legal frameworks. These frameworks seek to protect individuals from discrimination, arbitrary detention, torture, and other forms of human rights violations. They also aim to ensure that all individuals have access to necessities such as food, shelter, education, and healthcare.

The principle of human dignity has helped to shape the understanding of individual freedoms and liberties. It underpins the recognition of inherent rights, such as the right to life, liberty, and security of the person, the right to freedom of thought, conscience, and religion, and the right to equal protection under the law. Many international human rights instruments, such as the Universal Declaration of Human Rights, the International Covenant on Civil and Political Rights, and the Convention on the Elimination of All Forms of Discrimination Against Women, protect these rights.

The belief in the inherent worth and dignity of every individual has also sparked movements and activism aimed at challenging oppressive systems and advocating for equality. Throughout history, individuals and groups have fought against discrimination, racism, sexism, and other forms of injustice, inspired by the conviction that all humans deserve respect, fairness, and equal opportunities.

The belief that all humans are made in the image of God crucially influenced development and promotion of human rights ideologies. It underscores the importance of recognizing and respecting the inherent dignity and worth of every individual, regardless of their differences. This belief has shaped legal frameworks, inspired activism, and continues to drive efforts towards creating a more just and equitable world for all.

Justice and Law: Christian principles of justice, mercy, and fairness have shaped many legal systems, particularly in Western societies. These principles have had a significant impact on the development of laws and legal practices, influencing the core values and ideals upheld by societies.

For example, the concept of restorative justice, which aims to repair the harm caused by a crime through forgiveness and reconciliation, finds its roots in Christian teachings. Christian faith centers on forgiveness and redemption, and these principles have shaped legal frameworks to promote healing and restoration in crime-affected communities.

Restorative justice programs often involve bringing together the victim, offender, and community members to engage in open dialogue and address the harm caused and prevent future offenses. By incorporating Christian principles into the legal system, societies strive to balance punishment and compassion, seeking not only to hold individuals accountable for their actions but also to foster healing and reconciliation among all those involved.

Section 4: Art and Faith

Art and Literature: Christian themes have profoundly influenced art and literature throughout history, serving as a rich source of inspiration for countless masterpieces. One such example is Michelangelo's iconic Sistine Chapel, which showcases biblical scenes and figures with unparalleled grandeur and beauty. The frescoes on the chapel's ceiling, including the famous depiction of Adam and God's creation, have become enduring symbols of divine creation and the relationship between God and humanity.

In the realm of literature, Dante Alighieri's "Divine Comedy" stands as a monumental work that delves into the intricacies of Christian theology and the afterlife. Comprised of three parts–Inferno, Purgatorio, and Paradiso–Dante takes readers on a journey through Hell, Purgatory, and Heaven, exploring concepts of sin, redemption, and the divine order. His vivid descriptions and allegorical representations of various individuals and their fates have captivated readers for centuries, leaving an indelible mark on the literary landscape.

John Milton's epic poem "Paradise Lost" is another

masterpiece heavily influenced by Christian themes. The work explores the fall of man, drawing from the biblical account of Adam and Eve's expulsion from the Garden of Eden. Milton delves into profound theological questions, addressing themes of free will, temptation, and the nature of evil. Through his poetic prowess, Milton presents a complex narrative that challenges traditional perceptions of morality and human condition.

These works, among numerous others, have not only shaped cultural perceptions and narratives, but have also served as vehicles for contemplating profound philosophical and spiritual questions. The enduring influence of Christian themes in art and literature continues to resonate with audiences, offering insights into the human experience and providing a platform for exploring the depths of faith and belief.

Music and Rituals: Christian music, from hymns sung in traditional churches to contemporary worship songs played in modern gatherings, has played a significant role in shaping musical traditions and rituals within the Christian faith. Biblical teachings deeply root these musical expressions, which serve as meaningful spiritual communication and connection with God.

Christian music carries powerful themes of hope, faith, love, and worship, often drawing inspiration from sacred scriptures. These songs are not just a form of artistic expression, but are also integral to the communal identity and shared experience of believers.

Whether it is the majestic sound of an organ accompanying a hymn or the energetic rhythm of a contemporary praise song, Christian music serves as a unifying force, bringing individuals together in worship and celebration. It enhances the solemnity of rituals such as baptism and communion, providing a sonic backdrop that elevates the spiritual atmosphere.

Christian music also plays a crucial role in the gospel's proclamation, spreading the message of God's love and redemption to both believers and non-believers alike. Music has become an indispensable part of Christian rituals, serving as a powerful tool for expressing faith, fostering community, and deepening spiritual connection.

Social Movements

Abolition and Civil Rights: Many social movements, such as the abolition of slavery and the civil rights movement, were driven by Christian leaders and groups who interpreted their faith as a call to advocate justice and equality. These movements aimed to challenge and dismantle oppressive systems that perpetuated discrimination and inequality.

One notable figure in the abolitionist movement was William Wilberforce, a British Christian politician and philanthropist. Inspired by his religious beliefs, Wilberforce tirelessly campaigned against the transatlantic slave trade and played a crucial role in the passing of the Slave Trade Act of 1807, which abolished the slave trade in the British Empire.

Christian leaders, such as Martin Luther King Jr., heavily influenced the United States civil rights movement of the 1950s and 1960s. King, a Baptist minister, believed in the power of nonviolent resistance and drew inspiration from his Christian faith to fight against racial segregation and discrimination. He is best known for his role in organizing the Montgomery Bus Boycott and delivering his iconic "I Have a Dream" speech, which called for racial equality and justice.

These examples highlight how Christian leaders and groups have historically played a significant role in advocating for social justice and fighting against systemic injustices.

Environmental Stewardship: The Christian concept of stewardship, derived from the belief that humans are caretakers of God's creation, has inspired movements focused on environmental protection and sustainable living.

This concept encourages individuals and communities to take responsibility for the well-being of the planet and its resources. It emphasizes the idea that humans have a moral obligation to preserve and protect the environment for future generations.

As a result, many Christians have engaged in activities such as conservation, recycling, and advocating for policies that promote sustainable practices. In addition, churches and religious organizations have established initiatives and programs to educate their members about the importance of environmental stewardship and to provide resources for implementing eco-friendly practices in their daily lives.

These efforts not only align with the teachings of Christianity but also contribute to the broader global movement towards environmental sustainability. By integrating faith and environmental consciousness, Christians are playing a vital role in promoting a more harmonious relationship between humanity and the natural world.

Contemporary Influence.

Modern Ethical Debates: Christian values continue to play a crucial role in contemporary debates on a wide range of issues, including bioethics, social justice, and economic practices. These debates involve various ethical questions, such as the morality of genetic manipulation, the distribution of wealth and resources, and the treatment of marginalized communities. While it is important to note that different Christian denominations may hold diverse perspectives on these matters, the underlying influence of faith in these discussions is undeniably significant.

When considering bioethics, Christian values often shape the debate on topics such as abortion, euthanasia, and stem cell research. For example, many Christians believe in the sanctity of life and view abortion as morally wrong, while others may argue for the right to choose based on different interpretations of biblical teachings. Similarly, the question of euthanasia raises issues of compassion, dignity, and the potential interference with God's plan for each individual's life. Stem cell research, with its potential to address medical conditions and improve lives, also raises concerns about the destruction of human embryos and the ethical implications involved.

Social justice is another area where Christian values come into play. Jesus' teachings about love, compassion, and equality ground discussions of poverty, discrimination, and human rights. Christians are called to advocate for the marginalized and oppressed, seeking to create a more just and equitable society. However, there may be different interpretations and approaches within Christian denominations on how to address these issues, resulting in ongoing debates and discussions.

Economic practices and policies are also subject to ethical scrutiny from a Christian perspective. The biblical teachings on stewardship, generosity, and economic justice contribute to the conversation on wealth distribution, fair trade, and corporate responsibility. Some Christians argue for a more egalitarian economic system that prioritizes the well-being of all individuals, while others emphasize personal responsibility and the importance of free market principles. These differing viewpoints within Christian denominations add complexity to the ongoing ethical debates surrounding economic practices.

Interfaith Relations: Christianity's emphasis on love and peace influences its approach to interfaith dialogues and cooperation, promoting understanding and collaboration among diverse religious communities. In the pursuit of interfaith relations, Christians strive to foster an environment of respect and acceptance, recognizing the inherent dignity and worth of every individual regardless of their religious beliefs. They acknowledge that engaging in dialogue with people of different faiths can lead to a deeper appreciation of one's own beliefs, as well as a broader understanding of the diverse ways in which individuals seek connection with the divine.

Through interfaith cooperation, Christians aim to build bridges of understanding and work towards common goals, such as promoting social justice, peace, and the well-being of all people, regardless of their religious background. The teachings of Jesus Christ, who emphasized the importance of love, compassion, and inclusivity in all aspects of life, guide this approach.

By embracing these principles, Christians actively contribute to a more harmonious and tolerant society, where individuals of different faiths can come together in mutual respect and cooperation, fostering a world that celebrates diversity and promotes unity.

In summary, Christian values and beliefs have deeply permeated various aspects of cultural and societal life, shaping norms, behaviors, and institutions. These influences reflect both historical legacies and ongoing contributions to contemporary society. From art and literature to education and politics, Christianity has left an indelible mark on human civilization.

The Christian faith has inspired countless masterpieces of art, such as Michelangelo's Sistine Chapel frescoes and the works of Leonardo da Vinci. Christian themes and symbols have also found their way into literature, with authors like C.S. Lewis and J.R.R. Tolkien incorporating Christian allegories into their renowned works.

Christian teachings have played a crucial role in the development of education systems around the world, emphasizing the importance of moral values, compassion, and the pursuit of knowledge.

In the realm of politics, Christianity has influenced the formation of laws and governance structures, with concepts such as equality, justice, and human rights deeply rooted in Christian principles.

Christian institutions, such as churches, charities, and missionary organizations, have been at the forefront of social welfare, providing aid and support for those in need. Overall, the impact of Christian values and beliefs on cultural and societal life is undeniable, shaping the way people think, behave, and interact with one another.

7

Global Missions and Healthcare

I REMEMBER READING ABOUT a young nurse named Mary Thompson who volunteered with a faith-based mission called "Healing Hands" in the early 1900s. Inspired by her deep sense of compassion and desire to make a difference, Mary embarked on a life-changing journey to remote areas of Africa. With limited resources and facing numerous challenges, she selflessly dedicated herself to providing basic medical care to those in need and empowering local women to become skilled midwives.

Mary's mission involved traveling to some of the most underserved and isolated communities, where access to healthcare was virtually non-existent. Armed with her medical knowledge and a relentless determination, she tirelessly worked to heal the sick and ease suffering.

Through her efforts, she not only brought relief to count-less individuals, but also helped establish a foundation for sustainable healthcare within these communities.

In her letters home, Mary poured her heart out, vividly describing the resilience and gratitude she witnessed in the people she served. She spoke of mothers who had walked for days, carrying their sick children on their backs, just to receive her care. She shared stories of elderly men and women who, despite facing unimaginable hardships, still possessed an unwavering spirit of hope and faith. Mary's words painted a picture of a community that, despite their circumstances, remained determined to thrive and find joy in the simplest of things.

Mary's dedication went beyond just providing immedi-ate medical relief; she recognized the importance of equip-ping the locals with the skills and knowledge to sustain their own healthcare practices. She trained local women to become midwives, empowering them to take charge of childbirth and prenatal care in their communities. By doing so, Mary ensured that her impact would extend far beyond her time in Africa, creating a legacy of self-suffi-ciency and empowerment.

Mary's story serves as a powerful reminder of the transformative power of compassion and service. Her unwavering commitment to improving the lives of those she encountered is a testament to the indomitable human spirit and the profound impact that one individual can have on a community. Mary's legacy lives on, inspiring future generations to follow in her footsteps and make a difference in the lives of others.

Could you tell me why we do Missions? Could you tell me why do people put their lives in harm's way to minister to people in third-world countries who could never repay them?

The biblical mandate is clear - to spread the love and message of Jesus Christ to all nations. In Matthew 28:19-20, Jesus commands his disciples to "go and make disciples of all nations, baptizing them in the name of the Father and of the Son and of the Holy Spirit, and teaching them to obey everything I have commanded you." This Great Commission serves as the foundation for mission work.

Christians believe it is their duty to share the good news of salvation and serve those in need, regardless of the personal cost or lack of repayment. They are driven by compassion and the desire to make a positive impact on the lives of others, even in the most challenging and unfamiliar environments.

Missionaries often sacrifice their comfort, safety, and financial stability to bring hope, healing, and spiritual guidance to those who may have limited access to these resources. The act of selflessness and dedication showed by missionaries reflects their deep faith and commitment to fulfilling the teachings of Jesus. Ultimately, missions are a testament to the transformative power of love and the belief that every individual, regardless of their circumstances, deserves to experience God's grace and mercy.

I have had the privilege of serving on numerous mission teams, taking on leadership roles in most of these experiences. Over the years, I have ventured to countries across the globe, including Ecuador, Nicaragua, Honduras, Mexico, Cuba, Costa Rica, France, Spain, and beyond. Each mission trip has been a transformative journey, providing me with invaluable insights into the indomitable spirit of humanity amidst seemingly insurmountable challenges.

One of the earliest missions that deeply affected me was in Ecuador, where I witnessed firsthand the remarkable resilience of individuals facing extreme poverty and en-

vironmental adversity. The people I encountered in remote villages displayed an unwavering determination to
persevere, despite the aridity of their surroundings and the
destruction caused by natural disasters.

In Nicaragua, the strength and resourcefulness of communities grappling with political unrest and economic in-
stability moved me. Despite facing numerous obstacles,
the locals showed a remarkable ability to find hope and
joy amidst adversity. Their unwavering spirit and commitment to community upliftment left an indelible mark on
my heart.

Similarly, in Honduras and Mexico, I encountered communities plagued by violence and social inequality. However, it was inspiring to witness the unwavering determination of individuals who refused to succumb to despair.
Their resilience in the face of overwhelming challenges
served as a powerful reminder of the human capacity to
overcome even the most daunting circumstances.

My mission trips to Cuba, Costa Rica, France, and
Spain further broadened my perspective on the resilience
of human beings. The tenacity of Cuban society, which
has endured decades of economic sanctions while maintaining a vibrant culture and unwavering national pride,

struck me. In Costa Rica, I witnessed the remarkable resilience of communities affected by natural disasters, as they banded together to rebuild their lives and create a brighter future.

Each evening during my time in Cuba, I preached under a makeshift shelter. This resulted from the strict regulations imposed by Fidel Castro, the country's dictator, who prohibited any new church constructions. Despite this obstacle, our team dedicated ourselves to repairing their aged sanctuary, working tirelessly throughout the day. However, what struck me the most was the incredible spirit of the congregation. They were humble and contrite, embodying a genuine love that knew no bounds.

Their unconditional love extended towards us as they welcomed us into their community with open arms. The hospitality we received from the Cuban people was truly unforgettable. But it wasn't just their warm reception that left a lasting impact on me; it was the unwavering hope that radiated from each person's eyes. Despite the challenging circumstances they faced, their faith remained steadfast, and their hope in a better future was palpable. Cuba may have been a land of restrictions, but it was also a place where the human spirit thrived against all odds.

Venturing beyond the Latin American continent, my experiences in France and Spain introduced me to the resilience of individuals facing unique challenges. In France, I encountered communities grappling with social and economic inequality, yet witnessed the power of unity and collective action in effecting positive change. Similarly, in Spain, I learned about the resilience of the people in overcoming economic downturns and political turbulence.

These mission trips have been pivotal in shaping my worldview and instilling in me a deep appreciation for the strength of the human spirit. They have reinforced my commitment to serving others and have inspired me to continue seeking opportunities to make a positive impact on the lives of those facing adversity.

In Nicaragua, during our visit to the city of Leon, we found a heart-wrenching reality known as the "Dump People." These makeshift dwellings offered minimal protection against the relentless sun, torrential rains, and biting winds that plagued the area. The daily struggle for survival amidst the filth and squalor was a shocking testament to the dire circumstances that many people in Nicaragua face. The stench from constantly burning fires filled the lungs with a terrible pungency never witnessed by this missioner.

There, I also stood one day in an underground prison in Nicaragua that was specifically constructed by Daniel Ortega and the Sandanista's confining their political prisoners. This grim facility, known as El Chipote, served as a site of torture and terror during the Sandinista regime.

Designed to instill fear and crush dissent among those opposing the ruling party, the prison lay hidden beneath a nondescript government building. The underground cells were small, cramped, and devoid of natural light, creating an atmosphere of despair and hopelessness.

Metal clamps, cruel instruments used to restrain prisoners and inflict unimaginable pain, lined the walls. These clamps, embedded into the walls, served as harrowing reminders of the inhumane treatment endured by the inmates. Prisoners would be bound to these clamps, helpless and vulnerable, as they awaited their brutal fate.

Execution by gunfire was a common method employed by the Sandinistas to eliminate political opponents. Today, one can still see the haunting remnants of this violence: visible gunshot marks and dried bloodstains remain on the concrete walls. The abhorrent nature of the atrocities committed within this prison is so extensive that this concise article cannot adequately cover them. The stories of the survivors, however, serve as a testament to the resilience of the human spirit and a reminder of the importance of fighting for justice and freedom.

Global missions and healthcare refer to the efforts made by individuals, organizations, and governments to provide medical aid and support to populations in need around the world. These missions typically involve a range of activities, including providing medical care, conducting health screenings and assessments, administering vaccinations, and delivering essential medicines and supplies.

Global missions and healthcare aim to address the health disparities and challenges underserved communities, particularly in developing countries with limited access to quality healthcare, face. These initiatives often involve collaboration between local healthcare providers, international medical teams, non-governmental organizations, and governmental agencies to ensure the delivery of comprehensive and sustainable healthcare services. Through global missions and healthcare, the goal is to improve health outcomes, reduce mortality rates, and enhance the overall well-being of individuals and communities globally.

A brief history of global healthcare missions would entail the evolution and growth of efforts to provide medical care and support to underserved populations worldwide. Healers and physicians in ancient civilizations traced the concept of healthcare missions back to their travels to distant lands, offering knowledge and expertise. However, it was during the colonial era that healthcare missions gained significant momentum. European nations, particularly the British Empire, established medical facilities and sent physicians and nurses to their colonies to treat local populations and manage public health issues. These historic missions focused on providing basic healthcare services, such as vaccinations, primary care, and maternal and child health.

In the 19th century, religious organizations, particularly Christian missionaries, played a pivotal role in expanding global healthcare missions. Missionaries from various denominations established hospitals, clinics, and dispensaries in regions with limited access to medical care. Their efforts were driven by both religious and humanitarian motivations, aiming to alleviate suffering and promote the spread of their faith. These missions not only provided medical treatment but also focused on education and training, empowering local communities to take charge of their healthcare needs.

The 20th century marked a significant shift in global healthcare missions, as they became more diverse and multidimensional. Humanitarian organizations, such as Médecins Sans Frontières (Doctors Without Borders), emerged, bringing together medical professionals from different specialties to respond to emergencies and provide healthcare in conflict zones and disaster-stricken areas.

The World Health Organization (WHO) and other international bodies began coordinating and supporting global health initiatives, aiming to improve healthcare access and equity on a global scale.

Advances in transportation and communication technology further facilitated the expansion of global healthcare missions. Medical professionals could now travel more easily to remote areas and provide specialized care. Telemedicine also emerged as a powerful tool, enabling healthcare providers in underserved regions to diagnose and treat patients remotely.

Today, global healthcare missions continue to develop and adapt to the changing needs and challenges of the world. While the focus remains on delivering quality healthcare to underserved populations, missions increasingly incorporate community development, health education, and capacity building to create sustainable healthcare systems. Collaborative efforts between governments, non-governmental organizations, and local communities are now integral to the success of these missions, ensuring that healthcare services are culturally sensitive, accessible, and tailored to the specific needs of each population.

In conclusion, the history of global healthcare missions is a testament to the ongoing commitment of medical professionals and organizations to address the healthcare disparities that exist worldwide. From ancient healers to modern-day humanitarian efforts, the journey to provide equitable healthcare for all remains an ongoing endeavor rooted in compassion and the pursuit of social justice.

The role of various governments in supporting or regulating global healthcare missions is a crucial aspect of ensuring the provision of healthcare services worldwide. Governments play a significant role in supporting these missions by providing financial assistance, resources, and infrastructure to international healthcare organizations.

Healthcare initiatives in developing countries with limited access often receive government funding.

International organizations and governments can work together to create policies and guidelines for healthcare services. This includes ensuring the safety and quality of healthcare provided, as well as implementing measures to protect vulnerable populations. Governments also play a vital role in coordinating and facilitating the deployment of healthcare professionals and volunteers to areas in need. By providing support and regulation, governments contribute to the success and sustainability of global healthcare missions, ultimately improving the health and well-being of individuals and communities around the world.

There are numerous challenges and barriers that impact missions related to transportation, supply chain management, and infrastructure. One of the key challenges is ensuring efficient and reliable transportation for goods and personnel. This can be daunting in remote or inaccessible areas, where the lack of proper roads, airports, or seaports can hinder the movement of essential resources and equipment. The availability and maintenance of suitable vehicles and aircraft are crucial factors in the success of these missions.

Another significant obstacle is effective supply chain management. Coordinating the procurement, storage, and distribution of supplies, including food, water, medical equipment, and other critical resources, can be complex and challenging, especially in emergency or crisis situations. It requires careful planning, robust logistics systems, and strong communication networks to ensure that the right supplies reach the right place at the right time.

Inadequate infrastructure poses a significant barrier to mission success. In many regions, the lack of essential infrastructure, such as power grids, communication networks, and healthcare facilities, can severely limit the effectiveness of relief and development efforts. Without reliable infrastructure, it becomes difficult to establish and maintain the necessary facilities and services needed for sustainable development and response to crises.

Addressing these challenges and barriers requires comprehensive planning, collaboration among various stakeholders, and the utilization of innovative technologies and strategies. Governments, non-governmental organizations, and international bodies must work together to overcome these obstacles and create a conducive environment for effective transportation, supply chain management, and infrastructure development in mission-related activities.

In Venezuela, our mission team had to be canoed up the Apure River to witness to and administer healthcare to the natives in a small village where a missionary had lived for over 30 years. It was a river filled with piranha, and we were afraid to even touch our fingers in the water on our six-mile journey. We actually caught and ate some piranhas for dinner that evening! Great tasting fish!

To maximize cargo space, we loaded the supplies into each canoe as high as possible. It made it tough for our team to manage this, but we did with God's grace.

We also taught the native children a Vacation Bible School and their understanding astonished us. We knew then that it was definitely God's call upon our lives to be there in that place on the edge of the Amazon.

On one of our trips to Honduras, our team of medical volunteers embarked on a mission to provide much-needed healthcare services to the local communities. As part of our preparations, we carefully packed and organized a substantial amount of essential medical supplies, ranging from medications to medical equipment.

However, upon our arrival at the airport, we encountered an unexpected hurdle. The local officials, responsible for ensuring the safety and suitability of imported goods, held our medical supplies for five days. Their intention was to examine and thoroughly verify the quality and appropriateness of the supplies, ensuring that they met the standards to benefit the people of Honduras.

While this delay was initially frustrating, we understood the officials' commitment to safeguarding the health and well-being of their citizens. Despite the setback, we patiently awaited the clearance of our supplies, knowing that once approved, they would play a vital role in positively affecting the lives of the communities we aimed to serve. This is merely another supply chain issue missioners face while in a developing country.

The following are just a few success stories and the impact on people's lives.

1. Ebola Response in West Africa (2014-2016). Organizations like WHO and MSF played a critical role in controlling the outbreak through coordinated healthcare delivery, community engagement, and public health education.

2. The Carter Center's Guinea Worm Eradication Program. Sustained efforts have reduced the incidence of Guinea worm disease by over 99.99%.

3. The continuation of data showing improvements in health indicators, such as reductions in child mortality rates, increased vaccination coverage, and improved maternal health outcomes, is to be commended.

I recently learned about a doctor named Janice who works with Doctors Without Borders, an international humanitarian medical organization. Janice's passion for helping those in need drove her to work in conflict zones with limited medical care. She recounted a heart-wrenching experience of treating a young child severely injured by shrapnel during a violent conflict.

The child's wounds were critical and required immediate attention. Janice and her medical team worked tirelessly to stabilize the child's condition, performing life-saving surgeries and providing round-the-clock care. The child's recovery was nothing short of miraculous, a testament to the dedication and skill of the medical team. Despite the challenging circumstances, Janice and her colleagues were determined to provide the best possible care to their patients. The gratitude of the child's family was overwhelming, as they expressed their deep appreciation for the team's efforts in saving their loved one's life. Janice's story exemplifies the dedication of healthcare workers in war zones, who go to great lengths to help victims of violence.

A story that stands out is about a young woman named Aliana, who lived in a remote village in Ethiopia. Before the maternal health program, Aliana's community had extremely limited access to prenatal care. Pregnant women like Aliana often had to travel long distances to reach the nearest health facility, facing financial constraints and transportation challenges. As a result, many expecting mothers could not receive the essential care they needed, putting their own lives and the lives of their unborn babies at risk.

Fortunately, global missions, in collaboration with local healthcare providers, initiated a maternal health program in Aliana's village. The program aimed to improve access to prenatal care and ensure safe deliveries for women in underserved areas. As part of this initiative, the program trained community health workers to provide vital health-care services to pregnant women within their own communities.

Aliana was one of the fortunate women who directly benefited from this program. From the moment she discovered she was expecting, she received regular visits from a dedicated community health worker who monitored her health, provided necessary medical tests, and offered guidance on nutrition and healthy habits during pregnancy. Aliana's community health worker also ensured she had access to prenatal vitamins and medications, which were previously scarce in the village.

With the continuous support and guidance of her community health worker, Aliana's pregnancy progressed smoothly. Regular check-ups and timely interventions helped identify and address any potential complications early on, ensuring that both Aliana and her baby remained in good health throughout the nine months.

When the day finally arrived, Aliana safely delivered a healthy baby girl in the local health facility, with skilled healthcare professionals present to provide assistance. Aliana and her family felt immeasurable joy and relief knowing their baby had arrived safely thanks to the maternal health program.

The impact of this program extended beyond Aliana's individual experience. Growing trust in the village's healthcare system resulted from the program's success. More expectant mothers sought care. The program not only improved the health outcomes of mothers and babies but also empowered the community health workers, who became respected figures within the village, serving as role models and advocates for better maternal healthcare.

Aliana's story serves as a powerful reminder of the transformative impact that dedicated healthcare initiatives can have on the lives of individuals and communities. Through the maternal health program, Aliana and countless other women in Ethiopia have gained access to the care they deserve, ensuring safer pregnancies, healthier babies, and brighter futures for all.

I remember reading about a telemedicine project in India called "Virtual Doctors" where highly qualified doctors based in urban centers provide consultations to patients in remote villages through video calls. This innovative initiative aims to bridge the healthcare gap and ensure that quality medical care reaches even the most underserved areas.

One such patient, an elderly man named Mr. Sharma, who lives in a remote village, shared his heartwarming experience of how this telemedicine service transformed his life. Mr. Sharma had been suffering from chronic ailments for several years, and accessing medical care meant embarking on arduous journeys to the city, which were not only physically exhausting but also financially burdensome.

However, with introducing the telemedicine service, Mr. Sharma no longer had to endure these hardships. Instead, he could conveniently consult with a doctor from the comfort of his own home. The video calls allowed the doctor to assess Mr. Sharma's condition, review his medical history, and prescribe medications or treatment plans.

This newfound accessibility to healthcare not only saved Mr. Sharma from numerous trips to the city, but also improved his health significantly. Regular virtual consultations effectively managed his chronic ailments, and he experienced a noticeable improvement in his overall well-being. The telemedicine project in India undeniably shows how technology overcomes geographical barriers and positively affects countless individuals lacking access to quality medical care.

I read a heartfelt letter from a dedicated and compassionate volunteer who recently returned from a life-changing global mission in war-torn South Sudan.

In his moving letter, he passionately encouraged individuals from all walks of life to engage actively in making a positive impact on the world. Reflecting on his transformative experience, he emphasized how it had profoundly altered his perspective on life, instilling in him a deep sense of empathy and a burning desire to create meaningful change.

The volunteer's words resonated with the readers, as he vividly described the harsh realities he witnessed and the immense suffering endured by the local communities. This eye-opening encounter with the harsh realities of poverty, conflict, and displacement propelled him to take action and inspire others to do the same.

By sharing his powerful account, he hoped to motivate individuals to step out of their comfort zones, challenge their own beliefs, and commit themselves to making a tangible difference in the lives of those less fortunate. Ultimately, his letter served as a poignant reminder that each person possesses the capacity to positively impact the world, urging readers to embrace this opportunity and become agents of change.

*Contribute to a mission project.

*Volunteer to go on an upcoming mission trip.

*Support those who go in your name with your gifts.

The following organizations are legitimate and the funds collected go completely to the projects under their umbrellas:

1. **Doctors Without Borders**. Provides emergency medical aid in conflict zones and areas affected by natural disasters.

2. **World Health Organization (WHO)**. Directs and coordinates international health within the United Nations system.

3. **Partners in Health**. Works to bring modern medical care to those in the world's poorest communities.

4. **Bill and Melinda Gates Foundation**. Invests in global health initiatives, including vaccines and infectious disease prevention.

5. **Volunteers in Missions**. A mission arm of The United Methodist Church, sending mission trips to countries worldwide. Contact a local UMC for more information.

6. **The General Board of Global Ministries**. Missions outreach of The United Methodist Church. Supported by local churches.

These are only a few of the major movements affecting missions work around the world. May I ask how you will get involved?

8

Personal Stories and Testimonies

THIS CHAPTER ILLUSTRATES INSPIRING testimonials from people like us who confront life at work, at home, on the mission field, or simply while making friends. Perhaps you'll find yourself somewhere in one of them.

John's Epiphany on a Mountain: John, a self-proclaimed skeptic, had always questioned the existence of something greater than himself. Determined to find answers and clear his mind, he embarked on a life-changing adventure–hiking the Appalachian Trail. The journey was grueling, testing his physical endurance and mental resilience. Halfway through, as if testing his resolve, nature unleashed a fierce storm.

Faced with the elements, John sought refuge in a small

cave, the only shelter in sight. Inside the cave, thunder reverberated through the air, and the storm's raw power vibrated through every fiber of his being. In that moment, surrounded by the sheer force of nature, a profound peace washed over him, and he felt an inexplicable connection to something greater than himself.

It was as if the storm had stripped away his skepticism, leaving only a deep sense of awe and wonder. Emerging from the cave, John carried with him a newfound faith that has guided his life ever since that transformative experience on the mountain.

Rosemary's Redemption in Prison: Rosemary had a troubled past and ended up in prison for a series of poor decisions. One day, a fellow inmate named Sarah approached her and invited her to join a Bible study group that met every Wednesday in the prison's chapel. Initially resistant and skeptical, Rosemary was hesitant to participate in any activities that seemed religious or spiritual. However, curiosity eventually got the best of her, and she attended one of the group sessions.

That day, a warm and welcoming atmosphere greeted Rosemary as she walked into the chapel. The group comprised inmates from various backgrounds, all seeking solace and guidance through the scriptures. Led by a dedicated volunteer named Pastor Johnson, the Bible study group became a safe space where Rosemary felt a sense of belonging and acceptance she had never experienced before.

As the weeks went by, Rosemary immersed herself in the teachings of the Bible. She found solace in the messages of hope and redemption, which resonated deeply with her own longing for change and renewal. The scriptures showed her past mistakes did not define her, but had the potential to transform her life for the better.

Inspired by the kindness and support she received from her fellow inmates and Pastor Johnson, Rosemary's perspective on life shifted. She saw herself in a new light, as someone capable of forgiveness and redemption. Motivated by her own personal transformation, Rosemary dedicated her life to helping others find faith and hope within the prison walls.

Through her newfound purpose, Rosemary started various initiatives within the prison community. She organized workshops on personal growth and emotional healing, encouraging her fellow inmates to confront their pasts and embrace a brighter future. Rosemary's compassion and unwavering belief in the power of redemption became a beacon of hope for those who had lost faith in themselves.

Rosemary's journey in prison was not an easy one, but it was a testament to the transformative power of faith and the resilience of the human spirit. Despite her troubled past, she found redemption and a renewed sense of purpose through the Bible study group. Rosemary's story serves as a reminder that even in the darkest of places, hope and forgiveness can lead to profound change and a life filled with meaning.

Joe's Brush with Death: Joe, a 32-year-old software engineer, was in a serious car accident on a rainy evening. The collision's severe impact completely wrecked his car, leaving him unconscious and critically injured. Paramedics rushed him to the emergency room, where doctors tirelessly worked to stabilize his condition. However, Joe remained in a coma for several weeks, teetering on the edge between life and death.

During his time in the coma, Joe experienced something extraordinary. In the depths of his unconsciousness, he had vivid dreams that felt incredibly real. In these dreams, he found himself surrounded by a warm, comforting light that seemed to embrace him with an indescribable sense of love and peace. The experience was so profound that it transcended the boundaries of his physical body and touched the very core of his being.

When Joe finally awoke from his coma, he became overwhelmed by a flood of emotions and a deep sense of gratitude for being given a second chance at life. As he reflected on his experience, he couldn't help but feel that he had glimpsed into something beyond the realm of scientific explanation. He felt as if he had glimpsed the spiritual dimensions of existence.

Driven by his curiosity and the need to make sense of his extraordinary encounter, Joe embarked on a journey of self-discovery. He delved into various religious and philosophical traditions, exploring their teachings on spirituality, life, and the afterlife. As he immersed himself in the wisdom of different faiths, he found solace and a profound connection with his newfound spirituality.

Joe's brush with death had transformed him in ways he couldn't have expected. It had awakened within him a deep yearning for a higher understanding of life's mysteries. With each passing day, Joe continued to explore and embrace his spirituality, finding solace and purpose in his newfound beliefs. This extraordinary experience had not only granted him a second chance at life, but had also opened doors to a whole new realm of existence that he had never considered.

Sara's Unexpected Guide: Sara, a highly accomplished businesswoman, found herself at a crossroads in her life, sensing a void that her professional achievements couldn't fill.

It was during a business trip to India that fate intervened, leading her to a life-altering experience. Amid a vibrant and chaotic market, Sara became disoriented. Feeling a mix of panic and vulnerability, she was approached by an elderly woman who exuded an aura of wisdom and compassion.

Sensing Sara's distress, the woman kindly offered to guide her back to her destination. As they navigated through the bustling streets, the woman shared heartfelt stories of faith, love, and the pursuit of a purposeful existence. Her words resonated deeply with Sara, stirring something within her she had long neglected. The elderly woman's teachings illuminated the importance of cherishing moments, finding joy in the simplest of things, and embracing a life that held true meaning.

By the time they arrived at Sara's intended location, Sara felt an undeniable shift in her perspective, as though something had lifted a veil. This chance encounter ignited a profound journey of self-discovery and spiritual awakening for Sara, one that continues to shape her life to this very day. Filled with gratitude and newfound purpose, Sara embarked on a path of introspection, exploring her beliefs, values, and the intricate tapestry of her own soul. Through this unexpected guide, Sara found the missing piece of her existence and discovered a profound connection to something greater than herself, forever altering the trajectory of her life.

These stories remind us that faith can find us in the most unexpected places and through the most extraordinary circumstances. Whether it be a chance encounter with a stranger that offers a helping hand during a difficult time or a series of synchronicities that guide us towards our true purpose, faith has a way of showing up when we least expect it. In these moments, we remember the power of belief and the unseen forces working in our lives.

These stories serve as a testament to the resilience of the

human spirit and the ability to find hope and meaning even in the darkest of times. They inspire us to keep an open mind and heart, knowing that faith can manifest in ways we never could have imagined. So, as we navigate the difficulties of life, let us remain open to the possibility of faith finding us, guiding us, and transforming us in ways we never thought possible.

Faith in the Workplace

You've likely encountered numerous accounts illustrating how Christians successfully integrate their faith into their professional lives, skillfully navigating the often-challenging balance between career demands and their spiritual commitments. Let's look at a few illustrations to drive this concept home.

Robert's Integrity in Business

Robert is an entrepreneur who owns a small tech company called InnovateTech. From the very start, he founded his company on Christian principles, establishing its core values. Robert firmly believed integrity was paramount in business, and he strove to make his company known for its unwavering commitment to honesty and respect.

Robert always treated his employees fairly and respectfully. He believed that a positive work environment was crucial for productivity and growth, and he worked hard to create a supportive and inclusive culture within his team. Robert encouraged open communication, valued diverse perspectives, and promoted a sense of belonging among his employees.

Similarly, in dealing with clients, Robert always prioritized transparency and honesty. He believed in building long-term relationships based on trust, and he consistently delivered on his promises. Robert understood that maintaining integrity in business was not only the right thing to do ethically, but also essential for long-term success.

When faced with ethical dilemmas or tough decisions, Robert would often turn to his faith for guidance. He would seek counsel from his trusted faith community, pray for wisdom, and reflect on how his choices aligned with his Christian values. This approach not only helped him make sound decisions, but also ensured that his moral compass guided his actions.

Robert's commitment to integrity in business not only earned him a reputation for reliability and fairness, but also fostered a supportive and loyal team. His employees respected him not just as a boss, but also as a person of robust character. This created a positive work environment where everyone felt valued and motivated to contribute their best.

In conclusion, Robert's dedication to running his tech company with integrity has been a key factor in his success. By upholding Christian principles and treating both employees and clients with respect and honesty, he has built a company known for its ethical practices and unwavering commitment to doing what is right.

Emily's Compassion in Healthcare

Emily is a nurse who has always felt that her work is a calling from God. She makes it a point to pray for her patients and offer words of encouragement and hope, even in the most challenging situations. Her faith gives her the strength to provide compassionate care, and her patients often notice the difference.

Emily's dedication to her faith and profession has inspired many of her colleagues to approach their work with a similar sense of purpose and empathy. Throughout her career, Emily has encountered numerous challenging situations where patients are facing serious illnesses or undergoing painful treatments.

Despite the difficulties, Emily remains steadfast in her commitment to providing compassionate care. She takes the time to listen to her patients, offering a caring ear and a comforting presence. She understands that healthcare extends beyond physical treatment, and that emotional and spiritual support are equally important in the healing process.

Emily's faith is clear in her interactions with her patients. She often shares uplifting scriptures or offers words of encouragement, reminding her patients that they are not alone on their journey. Her patients often express gratitude for the difference Emily's compassion makes in their lives. Many have commented on the sense of peace they feel when she is by their side, providing care and offering prayers.

Beyond her direct patient care, Emily's dedication to her faith and profession has inspired many of her colleagues. They see her approach her work with a genuine sense of purpose and empathy, and it serves as a reminder to them of the importance of compassionate care. Emily's faith has created a ripple effect within her workplace, encouraging others to infuse their own work with a similar sense of meaning and compassion.

In conclusion, Emily's compassion in healthcare illustrates her deeply rooted faith. Her dedication to praying for her patients and offering words of encouragement and hope sets her apart as a nurse who truly cares. Her patients benefit from her unwavering commitment to their well-being, and her example inspires her colleagues. Emily's faith and profession intertwine to create a powerful impact on those around her, making her an exceptional healthcare professional.

Sophia's Creativity in Education:

Sophia is a high school teacher who is passionate about integrating her faith into her teaching practice. For Sophia, the classroom is more than just a place for academic learning; it is a mission field where she can make a positive impact on her students' lives. With a deep understanding of the power of education, Sophia strives to create an environment that is nurturing, inclusive, and values-driven.

Incorporating values such as kindness, integrity, and respect into her lessons, Sophia fosters an atmosphere where students feel safe to express themselves and explore their beliefs. She believes that by infusing her teaching with these core values, she can help her students develop not only academically but also ethically and morally.

Beyond her lessons, Sophia takes an active role in promoting her faith within the school community. She leads a student prayer group, providing a space for students who wish to deepen their spiritual journey. Sophia believes that by offering this outlet, she can support her students in their personal growth and provide them with a sense of community.

Sophia also encourages open discussions about faith and values in her classroom. By creating a safe and respectful environment, she facilitates conversations that allow her students to explore their own beliefs while also learning from one another. This approach fosters critical thinking, empathy, and understanding among her students, helping them to develop into well-rounded individuals.

Sophia's commitment to her faith has not only affected her teaching, but has also helped her build strong, trusting relationships with her students and their families. By modeling kindness, integrity, and respect, she has gained the trust and admiration of her students, who feel comfortable seeking guidance from her. Sophia actively engages with parents and guardians, fostering a collaborative partnership to support the holistic development of her students.

In conclusion, Sophia's creativity in education is clear through her intentional integration of faith, values, and open discussions into her teaching. Her commitment to creating a nurturing and inclusive environment has allowed her to make a positive impact on the lives of her students, helping them grow academically, ethically, and spiritually. Through her dedication and passion, Sophia continues to inspire and empower her students to become compassionate and responsible individuals who will make a difference in the world.

Faith can have an incredibly profound impact on individuals, guiding them through difficult times and providing a sense of purpose. Here are a few heartfelt stories of how faith has transformed lives:

Sarah's Journey of Healing: The loss of her mother to cancer plunged Sarah into a deep and overwhelming state of depression. The pain of losing her closest confidant left her feeling utterly lost and alone, with no idea how to navigate the turbulent emotions that consumed her. But in the darkest moments of her grief, Sarah found solace and support in an unexpected place - her faith community.

With a heavy heart and tears streaming down her face, Sarah sought refuge within the walls of her local church. It was there that she discovered the power of prayer, the comfort of counseling, and the unwavering love from her church family. Through countless hours spent in prayer, pouring her heart out to a higher power, Sarah felt a glimmer of hope amidst the darkness. She found that her faith provided her with the strength and resilience needed to face each day, even when it seemed impossible.

Embraced by the compassion and empathy of her church community, Sarah realized she was not alone in her pain. Others had experienced the heart-wrenching loss of a loved one to cancer, and they, too, were seeking healing and understanding. Inspired by her own journey, Sarah felt a calling to help others navigate their own path to healing.

Driven by her faith and a newfound sense of purpose, Sarah took it upon herself to start a support group within her community. This group provided a safe and nurturing environment where individuals could share their stories, find comfort in one another's experiences, and offer support during the most challenging times. Sarah's ability to listen and empathize, combined with her unwavering faith, became a guiding light for those who had lost their way.

Today, Sarah finds deep fulfillment in helping others find their own path to healing. Her support group has grown into a cherished community that provides solace and strength to countless individuals facing similar losses. Sarah's journey of healing not only transformed her own life, but has also become a beacon of hope for others who are searching for meaning and solace amid their own grief. Through her unwavering faith and the power of community, Sarah has discovered the true purpose of her own pain - to be a source of light and comfort for others on their own journey of healing.

John's Path to Recovery:

John had been battling with addiction for over a decade. His substance abuse had taken a toll on his relationships, causing rifts with family and friends, and had even cost him his job. He hit rock bottom when he found himself isolated and desperate for a way out. It was during this time that he made the courageous decision to seek help and enrolled in a faith-based rehabilitation program.

The rehabilitation program focused not only on addressing his addiction but also on providing spiritual guidance. John found solace in the teachings and support of fellow believers who had experienced similar struggles. The sense of community and understanding that he found within the program played a crucial role in his recovery journey.

John's faith became a guiding light in his path to sobriety. Through prayer, meditation, and regularly attending religious services, he found the strength and determination to resist the temptations of his addiction. His faith gave him hope and a renewed purpose, motivating him to mend broken relationships and rebuild his life.

Today, John is a living testament to the power of faith and recovery. He has transformed his own experience into a source of inspiration for others. As a counselor, he shares his story with those who are amid their own battles, offering guidance, empathy, and hope. John's unwavering faith in his higher power and his dedication to helping others has not only brought him personal fulfillment but has also made a positive impact on countless lives.

In his journey from addiction to recovery, John's faith has been the cornerstone of his transformation. It has allowed him to overcome the darkest moments and rebuild a life filled with purpose, love, and compassion.

Who are these people? Could you tell me why their stories resonate with us so much? Could it be that we have found ourselves in very similar situations? As we maneuver through this maze of experiences and events, we test our faith in God every day. A sustaining faith benefits us during challenges.

In our journey through life, we come across numerous individuals who captivate our attention and touch our hearts with their stories. These people could be ordinary individuals or renowned figures, but what makes them truly remarkable is their ability to connect with us on a deeply personal level. Their stories resonate with us because we see fragments of our own lives within their experiences.

We relate to their struggles, triumphs, and moments of vulnerability, realizing that we too have faced similar obstacles and emotions. As we navigate the complexities of existence, life constantly tests our faith in God. We encounter moments of uncertainty, despair, and doubt, seeking guidance and solace in our spiritual beliefs. The stories of these individuals remind us we are not alone in our journey. They serve as a source of inspiration and encouragement, reminding us that our faith is a powerful force that can sustain us through the most challenging of circumstances.

Community Support:

Faith communities play a vital role in offering support, encouragement, and fellowship to their members. Here are a few ways they make a difference:

1. **Emotional Support:** Faith communities often provide a safe space for individuals to share their struggles and receive empathy and understanding. This can be especially comforting during times of grief, illness, or personal challenges. Members offer prayers, words of encouragement, and a listening ear, helping individuals feel less alone.

2. **Practical Assistance:** Many faith communities organize volunteer groups and charitable activities to support those in need. This can include providing meals, financial assistance, transportation, or help with household tasks. The practical support offered by faith communities can significantly ease the burdens of daily life for their members.

3. **Spiritual Guidance:** Leaders and mentors within faith communities offer spiritual counseling and guidance, helping individuals navigate life's complexities with a sense of purpose and hope. This guidance can help members make important life decisions, find meaning in their experiences, and strengthen their faith.

4. **Sense of Belonging:** Being part of a faith community fosters a sense of belonging and connection. Regular gatherings, such as worship services, prayer meetings, and social events, create opportunities for fellowship and building strong relationships. This sense of community can boost mental and emotional well-being.

5. **Opportunities for Growth:** Faith communities often provide educational programs, workshops, and study groups that encourage personal and spiritual growth. These opportunities help members deepen their understanding of their faith, develop new skills, and strengthen their relationships with others.

6. **Encouragement and Motivation:** The collective spirit of a faith community can be incredibly motivating. Shared goals, communal prayers, and collective efforts toward common causes inspire members to pursue their aspirations with renewed vigor and determination.

Faith communities create a nurturing environment where individuals can find comfort, guidance, and a sense of purpose. Their support and encouragement can be life-changing, fostering resilience and personal growth.

9

The Future of the Church

WHERE DO WE GO from here as the Church of our Lord Jesus Christ? With voices on the right, the left, the middle, and the splits between Evangelical Christianity and mainline denominations, there is a clear sign the Church is in a state of transformation. As society develops and perspectives shift, inevitably, the Church will also undergo changes.

However, the future Church is not something we can predict with absolute certainty. The collective efforts of believers will shape it, guided by the teachings of Christ and the leading of the Holy Spirit.

The Church of the future may emphasize inclusivity and social justice, seeking to address the pressing issues of inequality, poverty, and environmental degradation. It may also embrace technology and digital platforms to enhance worship experiences and reach a wider audience.

The future Church may prioritize dialogue and unity, fostering collaboration among different Christian traditions and promoting understanding among diverse perspectives. Despite the uncertainties, one thing remains constant: the Church's mission to spread the love, grace, and salvation of Jesus Christ to all corners of the world.

Current Trends

We have known for the past twenty-five years that the church in America was declining. Recent studies and surveys have consistently shown a downward trend in the membership and influence of traditional denominations. Mainline Christianity, which includes churches such as the United Methodist Church, the Episcopal Church, and the Presbyterian Church (USA), has experienced a significant decrease in its membership, falling below the 50% mark over that period. Evangelical Christianity has witnessed a growth in its numbers, with more people identifying themselves as Evangelicals and becoming actively involved in Evangelical churches and movements.

However, amidst these shifting dynamics, a growing movement is currently operating under the name of "The Nones." This term refers to a group of individuals who do not identify with any religious denomination or affiliation. The rise of the Nones has been a notable phenomenon in recent years, as an increasing number of Americans are choosing to distance themselves from organized religion and embrace a more independent, individualistic spirituality. These individuals often describe themselves as spiritual but not religious, seeking personal connections with the divine outside of traditional religious institutions. I recently received discouraging news from a close friend of mine who lives in another state; he shared with me he had become disillusioned with mainstream Christianity and, as a result, he has joined the growing number of people who identify as religiously unaffiliated.

<u>U.S. Church Membership Falls Below Majority for First Time</u>

See: <u>https://churchtrac.com</u> and <u>https://baptist-news.com</u>

The reasons behind the decline of traditional Christianity and the rise of the Nones are complex and multifaceted. Some experts point to cultural shifts, such as an increasing focus on individualism and secularization, as contributing factors. Others argue that the church's failure to adapt to the changing needs and values of the younger generations has led to a disconnect between organized religion and the contemporary society.

As we navigate these changing religious landscapes, it becomes crucial to understand the various dynamics at play and explore innovative approaches to engage with individuals who identify as Nones. The future of Christianity in America will undoubtedly be shaped by the evolving religious preferences and beliefs of its citizens, and it is essential for churches and religious leaders to adapt and respond to these changing realities.

According to churchtrac.com, the church (as we know it) must adapt and innovate to remain relevant to the modern generation. We should take to heart everything discussed in this book to help the church become the church again. There is no room for failure at this point. Minds and hearts are being changed rapidly and we must be more open to listen to those who are leaving our churches and seek ways to collaborate with them.

It's clear that the landscape of the Church is shifting, and the rise of certain groups within Evangelical Christianity has certainly played a role in these changes. The tension between different theological and political perspectives can create divisions and challenges within the broader Christian community. However, it's also an opportunity for dialogue, reflection, and growth.

The future of the Church will probably depend on its ability to navigate these differences and find common ground. Embracing diversity, fostering understanding, and focusing on the core teachings of love, compassion, and justice can help bridge the gaps and create a more unified church.

Challenges the Church is Facing:

With declining attendance, aging leadership and pastoral leadership, and a reluctance to embrace change, the church is facing numerous challenges as it navigates the post-pandemic landscape. The dwindling number of congregants has raised concerns about the church's future viability and ability to sustain its mission.

The aging leadership within the church poses a challenge to adapt to developing societal trends and effectively connecting with younger generations. A shortage of diversity among pastoral leaders widens the gap between the church and its community's changing needs. The church's resistance to change and its adherence to traditional practices may hinder its ability to attract new members and meet the growing spiritual needs of the congregation.

Finally, generational shifts in beliefs and values have significantly affected the church's relevance and appeal, making it crucial for the church to find innovative ways to engage with younger audiences and foster a sense of inclusivity and acceptance.

Despite these uphill battles, it is imperative for the church to embrace adaptation and actively seek solutions to address these challenges in order to thrive in the ever-changing religious landscape.

Community Outreach: Many churches have recognized the importance of giving back to their communities and have started community outreach programs. These programs provide platforms for members to take part actively in various volunteer activities, using their unique skills and talents.

One such example is the organization of a weekly soup kitchen, where church members come together to prepare and serve nutritious meals to those in need. This not only helps to address the immediate physical needs of individuals experiencing hardship, but it also fosters a sense of purpose and belonging within the church community. By engaging in such outreach efforts, churches can create positive affects on the lives of those they serve while simultaneously strengthening the bond among their volunteers.

Youth Programs: Churches often run a variety of engaging and enriching youth programs that aim to provide a safe and supportive environment for young people within the community. These programs go beyond just religious education and incorporate a wide range of activities to cater to the diverse interests and talents of the youth. From sports leagues and competitions to music classes and choir groups, these programs offer an opportunity for young members to explore and develop their skills in a fun and nurturing setting.

Organizers often create study groups and educational workshops to help youth excel academically and foster a love for learning. The emphasis on building lasting friendships is a key aspect of these programs, as they encourage interaction and camaraderie among the participants. Through these youth programs, churches aim to instill important values such as teamwork, respect, and compassion, while also providing a platform for young individuals to express themselves and grow into well-rounded members of society.

Bible Study Groups: Small group Bible studies are a

common way for church members to deepen their faith and understanding of scripture. These groups often meet weekly, fostering close-knit communities where members can share their insights and support each other on their spiritual journeys.

These study groups typically comprise around 8 to 12 participants, creating a comfortable environment for open discussions and personal connections. They may gather in homes, church buildings, or online platforms, depending on the preferences and availability of the members. A facilitator who guides the group through a specific passage or theme from the Bible leads each session. The facilitator may provide study materials, such as commentaries or study guides, to enhance the understanding and exploration of the scriptures.

Bible study groups aim to promote a deeper understanding of God's word, encourage personal reflection, and foster a sense of community and accountability among its members. Besides studying the Bible, these groups often engage in prayer, worship, and other spiritual practices to further enrich their faith journeys.

Through the sharing of personal experiences and perspectives, participants gain unique insights and interpretations, allowing for a broader understanding of the scriptures. These small group Bible studies provide a safe space for individuals to ask questions, seek guidance, and grow in their relationship with God and each other.

Support Networks: Many churches offer support groups for individuals facing various life challenges, such as grief, addiction, or divorce. These groups provide a safe and confidential space for people to share their experiences and receive emotional and spiritual support from others who understand their struggles.

Trained facilitators who provide guidance and facilitate discussions typically lead these support groups. They offer a non-judgmental environment where individuals can freely express their thoughts and feelings without fear of criticism or rejection.

These support networks often incorporate elements of faith and spirituality, allowing participants to explore their beliefs and find solace in their religious practices. The supportive community created within these groups can help to help individuals navigate their difficult circumstances and find hope and healing.

These support networks often extend beyond the group meetings, as participants form strong bonds and develop lasting friendships. This sense of belonging and connection can provide a valuable source of ongoing support and encouragement in times of need. Overall, church support groups offer a valuable resource for individuals seeking understanding, guidance, and companionship on their journey towards personal growth and well-being.

Mentorship Programs: Churches often have mentorship programs in place to foster personal and spiritual growth among their members. These programs typically involve pairing older, more experienced individuals with younger members who are seeking guidance and support. The mentors play a crucial role in providing wisdom, encouragement, and a sense of belonging to their mentees.

Through regular meetings, one-on-one conversations, and shared activities, the mentors help the younger members navigate various aspects of their lives, including their faith journey. They offer insights and advice based on their own experiences, helping the mentees gain clarity and perspective.

The mentorship relationships formed within these programs can have a profound impact on the mentees, as they receive not only practical guidance but also emotional support and a sense of community. The mentors serve as role models, demonstrating what it means to live a life of faith and inspiring their mentees to strive for personal growth and spiritual maturity.

Overall, mentorship programs within churches create an environment where individuals can connect, learn from one another, and grow together in their faith.

If the church is to return to its original and true source, it must reexamine its core principles and teachings. We must trace the church back to early Christianity, when Jesus Christ and his disciples founded it. This entails studying the Scriptures, particularly the New Testament, which provides the foundation of Christian doctrine and practice. By carefully analyzing the teachings of Jesus and the writings of the apostles, the church can rediscover its authentic identity and purpose.

It is essential to study the history of the early church, understanding the challenges it faced and the ways it navigated through them. This historical perspective can shed light on the practices and traditions that have shaped the church over the centuries. The church, by returning to its original and true source, aligns itself with the timeless truths of the Gospel and roots its teachings and actions in the teachings of Jesus Christ.

Archaeological findings have shed light on early Christian practices and communities. For instance, the discovery of ancient Christian symbols, such as the ichthys (fish) symbol, and early Christian texts, like the Dead Sea Scrolls, offer valuable insights into the beliefs and rituals of early Christians. Early Christians commonly used the ichthys symbol, representing Jesus Christ as the "fisher of men," to identify themselves and their faith.

The Dead Sea Scrolls, discovered in the mid-20th century near the Dead Sea, contain various texts, including biblical manuscripts and other writings that provide a glimpse into the religious practices and beliefs of Jewish communities during the time of Jesus. These discoveries have enhanced our understanding of the early Christian movement and its development.

Discoveries in regions like Jerusalem, Bethlehem, and Nazareth have provided a richer understanding of the cultural and historical contexts in which biblical events occurred. Excavations in these areas have unearthed artifacts, structures, and inscriptions that provide a valuable context for the stories and teachings found in the Bible. For example, the discovery of ancient tombs and burial practices in Jerusalem has shed light on the cultural customs surrounding death and burial during biblical times. These findings help believers and scholars alike to better understand the environment and circumstances of the life of Jesus and the early church.

Connection to Sacred Sites: Excavations at sites considered sacred in Christianity, such as the Church of the Holy Sepulchre in Jerusalem, have confirmed their historical significance and provided new information about their construction and use over the centuries. People believe the Church of the Holy Sepulchre is the site of Jesus' crucifixion, burial, and resurrection, making it one of the holiest sites in Christianity. Archaeological investigations at this site have revealed different layers of construction and modifications, reflecting the continuous veneration and importance placed on this sacred location throughout history.

The discoveries of relics, artifacts, and inscriptions at the Church of the Holy Sepulchre have provided valuable insights into the religious practices and traditions associated with this significant place of pilgrimage for Christians worldwide.

Overall, archaeological research has contributed to our understanding of ancient Christian practices, biblical contexts, and the significance of sacred sites. By studying the material remains of the past, we can gain a deeper appreciation for the historical and cultural contexts in which Christianity emerged and developed.

The church's vision for the future can vary widely depending on the denomination, leadership, and the specific community it serves. Many churches aim to:

1. **Expand Outreach and Evangelism**: Engaging with the local community and beyond to share their faith and provide support to those in need.

2. **Promote Social Justice**: Addressing issues such as poverty, inequality, and environmental stewardship.

3. **Strengthen Community**: Building a strong sense of fellowship among members and creating a welcoming environment for newcomers.

4. **Embrace Modern Technology**: using digital tools to reach a broader audience through online services, social media, and other tech innovations.

5. **Youth and Family Focus**: Investing in programs that support young people and families, helping them grow in their faith and navigate life's challenges.

6. **Interfaith Dialogue**: Promoting understanding and cooperation between different religious traditions.

The church's mission, plans, and goals show what it believes and wants to achieve.

Since I have been a minister in both the United Methodist Church and in a Southern Baptist Church, I have done the research and give you here the future hopes of both churches. I list the links to these below each church, both United Methodist and Southern Baptist.

Let's look at the visions for the future of both the United Methodist Church and the Southern Baptist Convention.

United Methodist Church

The United Methodist Church's vision focuses on **"Making disciples of Jesus Christ for the transformation of the world"**. Their vision includes:

Community Outreach: At our church, we actively

address pressing social issues such as hunger, disease, and poverty. Through various outreach programs, we aim to extend God's grace and love to all members of our community. Our dedicated team works tirelessly to organize food drives, provide medical assistance, and offer support to those in need. We firmly believe in the power of community and strive to create a safe and inclusive space for everyone.

Global Mission: As followers of Christ, we understand the importance of engaging in international missions and social justice initiatives. We actively seek opportunities to partner with organizations around the world to make a positive impact on global issues. Our commitment to spreading God's love beyond our local community involves advocating for human rights, supporting education in underprivileged areas, and taking part in disaster relief efforts.

Inclusivity and Unity: We believe that a strong and vibrant church is one that embraces diversity and fosters unity among its members. Our church strives to create an environment where everyone feels welcomed, accepted, and valued. We actively work towards breaking down barriers and overcoming prejudices, striving for a more inclusive and unified church. Through intentional dialogue, education, and community-building events, we aim to build bridges and promote understanding among people of different backgrounds, cultures, and beliefs.

Youth and Family Engagement: We recognize that the youth and families are the future of our church and society. Therefore, we prioritize programs that support and nurture young people and their families. Our vibrant youth ministry offers a variety of engaging activities, such as youth groups, retreats, and leadership development opportunities. We also provide resources and support for parents, equipping them with the tools they need to raise their children in a loving and God-centered environment. We believe that investing in the well-being and spiritual growth of our youth and families is essential for a thriving church community.

References:

https://www.resourceumc.org

https://www.ministrymatters.com

Southern Baptist Convention

The Southern Baptist Convention's vision, known as **Vision 2025,** is a bold and ambitious plan to spread the message of Jesus Christ to every person. In order to achieve this goal, the Convention has outlined several strategic actions that they will undertake.

Increasing Missionaries: First, they aim to increase the number of missionaries by adding 500 full-time, fully funded missionaries to their ranks. These missionaries will be on the front lines, spreading the gospel and working to bring people to Christ.

Church Planting: The Convention plans to expand their presence by adding 6,000 new churches to their family. These new churches will serve as beacons of faith in communities across the nation, providing a place for worship and spiritual growth.

Youth Engagement: The Convention also prioritizes youth engagement, recognizing the importance of reaching and baptizing teenagers. They are committed to reversing the decline and teaching young people about Christ.

Cooperative Giving: The Convention aims to increase their annual giving to surpass $500 million through the Cooperative Program. This program allows churches to pool their resources and support missions and ministries both locally and globally. By increasing their giving, the Convention hopes to have an even greater impact on the world and share the love of Christ with those in need.

Overall, both the Southern Baptist Convention and the United Methodist Church denominations are united in their commitment to expanding their reach, engaging with communities, and powerfully promoting their faith. Through their strategic actions and unwavering dedication, they are working tirelessly to fulfill their mission to bring every person to Jesus Christ.

References:

https://www.baptistpress.com

https://www.absc.org

10

Summary of Our Work

L ET ME QUOTE AGAIN the Great Commission of Christ given to His disciples before his departure into heaven. This book you hold highlights the importance of this commission, found in Matthew 28:18-20.

"And Jesus came and spake unto them, saying, All power is given unto me in heaven and in earth. Go ye therefore, and teach all nations, baptizing them in the name of the Father, and of the Son, and of the Holy Ghost: Teaching them to observe all things whatsoever I have commanded you: and, lo, I am with you alway, even unto the end of the world. Amen."

In the Gospel of Matthew, Jesus spoke to his disciples, declaring the immense authority bestowed upon him both in heaven and on earth. With this authority, he commanded his followers to go forth and spread his teachings to all nations. This command included the instruction to baptize individuals in the name of the Father, the Son, and the Holy Ghost.

Jesus emphasized the importance of teaching these nations to observe and obey all the commandments he had given. In his parting words, he assured his disciples that he would be with them always, even until the end of the world. It is crucial that we recognize the gravity of this message and its relevance in the lives of our churches today. By revisiting the Great Commission, we can reestablish its vital role in our faith and recommit ourselves to carrying out this divine mandate.

We began this work by describing the relevance of exploring faith in today's world. Throughout these pages, we have sought to do just that from the Christian point of view.

Chapter One dealt with the role of faith in times of crises. The chapter highlighted examples of people of great faith who, despite facing significant challenges and trials that tested their beliefs, remained steadfast in their convictions and persevered. We explored how Christian communities have found strength during challenging times.

Chapter Two discussed persecution and our modern-day martyrs. We also related stories of Christians around the world facing dangers because of their commitments.

Chapter Three explored our environmental stewardship and the Christian's call to care for creation.

Chapter Four addressed the issues of social justice and human rights and the role of the church in promoting them.

Chapter Five was about technology, ethics, and our digital evangelism today and how each affects our lives and the church.

Chapter Six explained our cultural connections and pop culture, emphasizing the representation of Christian themes in movies, music, and literature. We looked at interfaith dialogues and their importance in the church's life in the future.

Chapter Seven dealt with the themes of global missions and healthcare and the challenges of missionary work in remote areas.

Chapter Eight highlighted personal stories and testimonials that warmed the heart and hopefully inspired our faith journeys. We discussed integrating faith into professional life.

In Chapter Nine, I outlined what I saw as the future of the church—where we have been and where we are going.

There are two appendices following this document that will provide you with more reference books for further studies. These reference books are specific to each chapter, offering additional resources to enhance your understanding of the subject.

Additionally, the second appendix contains a section that poses thought-provoking questions for further study. These questions encourage critical thinking and help you delve deeper into the topics discussed throughout the document.

It is my heartfelt thanks to you for purchasing this book and hopefully using it in your church Sunday School classes, in Bible Study groups, or in sermons from the pulpit. May God richly bless and keep you on your journey through life.

11

Appendix I: Books for Further Study

Books on Faith and Spirituality:

1. **"The Case for Christ"** by Lee Strobel: A journalist's investigation into the evidence for Jesus.

2. **"Mere Christianity"** by C.S. Lewis: A classic work discussing the fundamentals of Christian faith.

Books on Environmental Stewardship:

1. **"Serve God, Save the Planet"** by J. Matthew Sleeth: A call for Christians to embrace environmental stewardship.

2. **"The Green Bible":** Contains essays and passages highlighting the connection between faith

and care for creation.

Books on Social Justice and Human Rights:

1. **"Generous Justice"** by Timothy Keller: Explores how the Gospel compels Christians to seek justice and mercy.

2. **"The Hole in Our Gospel"** by Richard Stearns: Addresses the role of Christians in combating poverty and injustice.

Books on Technology and Ethics:

1. **"The Tech-Wise Family"** by Andy Crouch: Discusses how Christian families can navigate the digital age.

2. **"God, Technology, and the Christian Life"** by Tony Reinke: Examines the relationship between technology and Christian faith.

Books on Modern-Day Persecution:

1. **"The Insanity of God"** by Nik Ripken: True stories of faith and persecution from around the world.

2. **"Foxe's Book of Martyrs"** by John Foxe: A historical account of Christian martyrs.

Books on Digital Evangelism:

1. **"Platform: Get Noticed in a Noisy World"** by Michael Hyatt: Provides insights on using digital platforms for evangelism.

2. **"Irresistible: Reclaiming the New that Jesus Unleashed for the World"** by Andy Stanley: Discusses how to make the message of Jesus compelling in the digital age.

These books offer a wealth of knowledge and perspectives that can enrich your study.

12

Appendix II: Questions for Study Groups

CHAPTER **O**NE:

1How do faith communities respond during historical crises (e.g., plagues, wars)?

2. List any faith-driven responses to such natural disasters, pandemics, and economic hardships in the life of your church or another church.

3. What is your personal testimony on how you have found strength and hope through your faith during challenging times?

4. Analyze the importance of prayer, worship, and other faith practices that provide comfort and resilience during a crisis.

Chapter Two:

1. Could you name any modern-day martyrs?

2. Describe what persecution means to you.

3. How was Jesus persecuted? Could you discuss the trial he endured before his crucifixion?

4. Explore the strength and resilience of persecuted Christians, emphasizing their unwavering faith despite hardships.

Chapter Three:

1. Discuss the biblical basis for environmental stewardship and your understanding of how this impacts our world today.

2. What sorts of things are you doing to combat climate change?

3. Use the concepts of community gardens, clean-up projects, and sustainable practices to

discuss your views.

4. What actions can you take to affect individual actions and lifestyle changes to align with environmental stewardship principles?

Chapter Four:

1. In your words, what is social justice? Should it be a universal concept?

2. What are your human rights? How many can you list?

3. Discuss human trafficking, including its causes, effects, and the church's role in combating it.

4. What are your views on homelessness? Do you know a homeless person?

5. How may you advocate more for social justice and human rights?

Chapter Five:

1. What are your views on modern technologies and

how they affect today's world?

2. Discuss the ethical implications of AI, considering both the potential benefits and moral dilemmas.

3. How do churches use technology for worship services, outreach, and community building? Does your church use these methods? If not, why not?

4. What are your concerns about digital evangelism?

5. How can we balance tradition and innovation with traditional faith practices?

Chapter Six:

1. Analyze the portrayal of Christian themes in movies, music, and literature, noting positive and negative representations.

2. Discuss the importance of interfaith dialogues in promoting peace, understanding, and cooperation among different faith communities.

3. Reflect on how Christian values and beliefs influence cultural norms and societal behaviors.

4. What is the relationship between art and faith? Highlight artists who incorporate Christian themes into their work.

Chapter Seven:

1. Summarize missionary work in remote areas, including the challenges and rewards. Has your church sponsored mission trips?

2. Describe what you have learned about medical missions.

3. How could you be more involved in local and world missions?

4. Discuss how missions can promote sustainable development and long-term improvements in the communities they serve.

Chapter Eight:

1. Which inspiring testimonies blessed you the most? Which ones do you identify with?

2. Discuss how Christians integrate their faith into their professional lives.

3. Reflect on the role of faith communities in providing support, encouragement, and fellowship among people.

4. In what ways does your church respond to these needs?

Chapter Nine:

1. What do you see as the future of the church?

2. What are the current trends and predictions of the church?

3. What challenges does the church face today?

4. What is YOUR vision for the church's future? What would you like to see the church doing in our world today?

TO ORDER OTHER BOOKS BY DR. CRAVEY

https://drcharlescravey.com

or

Amazon, Books a Million, Barnes & Noble

Made in the USA
Columbia, SC
11 March 2025

54904669R00157